<u>ABOUT THE</u>

Renee has studied health and healing for over twenty years and holds a bachelor of science in human services from Upper Iowa of Wisconsin. She has nutrition and health coach training certification through the Institute for Integrative Nutrition, and is also a Life Strategies Coach in the areas of psychological health and well-being. She lives in Prairie du Sac, Wisconsin.

• • •

"I dedicate this book to you Dad. It is because of your role in my life and your early death that lead me down the path of healing and wellness. You are missed and always loved."

• • •

I would like to thank my best friend and husband Matthew and our two beautiful children, Emily and James for supporting my book writing venture. I would also like to thank Luke Dederick for creating the awesome cover illustration and Barb Cowsert and Kelly Klawitter Thomas for graciously editing my book.

Cover Design by JenGraphicDesigns.com

CONTENTS

Disclaimer

This book has been written and published strictly for informational purposes, and in no way should be used as a substitute for consultation with a medical doctor or health care professional. Do not consider educational material herein to be the practice of medicine or to replace consultation with a physician or other medical practitioner. The author and publisher are providing you with information in this work so that you can have the knowledge and can choose, at your own risk, to act on that knowledge. The author and publisher also urge all readers to be aware of their health status and to consult health professionals before beginning any health program, including changing dietary or nutrition habits. This book is not intended as a substitute for the medical advice of physicians. The reader should regularly consult a physician in matters relating to his/her health and particularly with respect to any symptoms that may require diagnosis or medical attention.

The author has made every effort to trace copyright owners. Where she has failed, she offers her apologies and undertakes to make proper acknowledgement where possible in reprints.

Preface

"The best project you'll ever work on is you." ~ Sonny Franco

I've studied health and healing for over twenty years and hold a bachelor of science in human services. I am certified as a nutrition and health coach through the Institute for Integrative Nutrition and am also a Life Strategies Coach in the areas of psychological health and well-being.

Human mind chatter creates emotional reaction and behavior that is complex and intriguing. Earlier in my life I struggled on a roller coaster of emotions including anger, anxiety, perfectionism, control issues and a self-defeating internal dialogue. Anxiety attacks developed after my Dad died at the age of 51. I was 29 and my first child was 18 months old.

My Dad's death became my "rite of passage". This is not in any way meant negatively. Seeing my Dad deteriorate before my eyes over the years and die at such an early age started my life on a new journey that lead me on a path of self-discovery and healing.

Sometimes circumstances, experiences and events force us into spiritual and personal growth and development. This is "the rite of passage" my Dad gave to me. When losing a loved one, our very foundation is shaken and we can be forced to explore everything we believed as our truth. Much of our truth doesn't even belong to us. It has been passed down from generation to generation or created within cultures, religions, politics and society as a whole. Conditioned beliefs are often very misleading and many are simply not true.

The journey of self-discovery or self-mastery isn't easy, quick or unpainful. It takes persistence, practice and unwavering belief in yourself. It takes determination and discipline on a daily basis. However, each small successful step is extremely rewarding along the never ending process of awakening. The process of discovering your authentic self is through forgiveness, self-acceptance and learning to love the whole of who you are. This process includes discovering false and limiting beliefs, as well as healing self-destructive thinking that creates unpleasant emotions and confrontational behaviors. The process of releasing your issues allows you to resonate with the unwavering truth about who you really are as a human-being, your life's purpose and why you are here.

Having dealt with a psychiatrist and counselor at a couple different points in my earlier life, I became dismayed by the labeling and standardization of limiting individuals to an all-encompassing box. Each of us has our depth, circumstances, pain, insecurities and personal experiences that cannot be boxed in a diagnosis or label. Psychiatry leaves out the spiritual aspect of an individual. Much emotional suffering comes from the suppression of the human soul, the absence of our spiritual nature, the ability to master ourselves and our mind.

Chapter 1: Which Reality Are You Living?

There are two realities of existence: the "internal" and the "external". The first is not focused on enough within our societal, community, education, religion or family structure. The "internal" reality is a process of going within, the process of self-mastery. Internalization promotes an individual's awareness of personal responsibility and how beliefs and actions contribute to all circumstances and life experiences. Where belief is a formulation of thought perception, truth comes from a knowingness through intuition. Internal reality leads to freedom, power and feeling of increased worth and purpose in life.

The other is commonly experienced as an "external" reality, an imposed reality. The external reality rides on a desire to obtain success and meaning through following the process of mandated systems and rules created by man-made structures within society. This process is a form of conformity that currently supports personal success as a result of defining oneself through showing accomplishments such as educational levels, monetary wealth, physical ability, appearance, material accumulation and socioeconomic status. Our accomplishments are what we have done. Achievements are external factors of how we define ourselves.

The internal discovery of purpose and worth (self-mastery) is far more rewarding than any external projection of success or status. Living a comfortable life or enhancing acquired skills should become a personal objective instead of a need to define oneself.

Knowledge comes from the external world and wisdom comes from within, the internal world. They are two very separate states of being. Knowledge is information one acquires from outside sources such as school, culture, personal experience and others' experiences. Wisdom is an inner knowingness beyond the formulation of beliefs and thoughts created in the mind. Knowledge does not necessarily produce internal growth and development. Internal growth and development come from "wisdom" acquired within. Wisdom begins with an understanding that speaks of personal responsibility and perseverance. Internal projections or self-dialogue ultimately create our life circumstances and personal realities whether pessimistic or optimistic. Wisdom strengthens one's internal sense of self, concurrently altering life experiences constructively within our reality. The external projections are an illusion of who we really are. Self and mind-mastery is the only way to find inner contentment, love for yourself and the ability to truly love others.

Beginning the process of internalization is not easy, but the progressing results are remarkable and in a sense unexplainable because they are a personal experience. Internal experiences can't be explained fully. The benefits I have realized have guided me to the desire to help others find the same understanding and experience of discovering inner-contentment and self-acceptance, no matter what accomplishments or socioeconomic status a person holds or doesn't hold.

This book is about self-observation, self-discovery and questioning the world around us. It is important to remember that we never stop growing, changing or learning: it is a lifelong process. Mastering the self and the mind isn't about putting yourself above or having more value or worth over others. The more you learn about your internal self, the more compassion and love you will have for others. The more you learn about yourself, the more purpose, worth and equality you will see in others. The more you know yourself, the more you will increase your ability to sense balance or imbalance in others. A self-care focus is about being accountable for every aspect of your life and how you reflect who you are onto the world.

If you are looking for something easy and quick, this book is not for you. Self-mastery comes from within and looking within often times can be painful or uncomfortable. You will not find self-discipline and healing in external forces and nobody can do the work for you. Keep in mind that none of us can be complete or faultless all the time. We are humans and we all carry a shadow side when events trigger emotions that throw us off from time to time. But the more you work on yourself, the easier it becomes to move through these trials and tribulations. Learning to laugh at challenging times also brings light and neutrality.

You will find repetition of words and even sentences throughout this book. Repetition is how we have been conditioned to react with emotions that were created from our thinking. Repetition can also reverse destructive thinking, emotions and behaviors. With each tip given in every chapter, find what resonates with you. Not every tip may be right for your particular energy or even perspective. Just be open to the information for you might come back to it with each new life passage.

Chapter 2: Our Thinking Connection

"When every thought absorbs your attention completely, when you are so identified with the voice in your head and the emotions that accompany it that you lose yourself in every thought and every emotion, then you are totally identified with your mind." ~ Eckhart Tolle

Whether our thinking has a positive disposition or a negative undertone, our thoughts contribute to our perceived reality and overall health. It was discovered through the testing of brain patterns that when a person indulges in a negative thought their brain chemicals begin to change. So what does this mean when considering our health? If our thinking creates chemical changes within our brain, could our thoughts also produce healing or even perpetuate physical and mental illness? Thought creates feelings and feelings create actions. Perception, feelings and actions create and maintain the health or dysfunctions of the body, mind and spirit.

Optimistic thinkers focus on finding solutions while pessimistic thinkers tend to dwell on problems. Pessimistic people argue with others as an attempt to take away others' power while consciously or unconsciously creating negativity and drama. This is how they feed their energy banks. They have cut themselves off from the free flowing energy source of love and compassion. Positive people generate love, offer new information and uplift others. They have an abundance of energy and can freely share it with others.

Focusing on personal or circumstantial issues perpetuates negative thinking, simultaneously influencing our emotions and stress level. Stress has been known to produce or exacerbate physical illness, charge emotions and mental health problems. Establishing emotional health, or even having a motivation to change, creates an appreciation for physical care, simultaneously influencing healthy eating and routine exercise habits. Acquiring the ability and stamina to control what we generate from our thought process either persuades balance or depresses our "feel good" emotions.

Emotional health is the ability to choose and control emotional reaction through controlling thought. When emotion is controlled through maintaining a healthy perspective, particularly in adverse situations, we avoid engaging in self-destructive behavioral patterns such as anger, resentment or hatred. Emotional reactions are an internal option produced by thoughts. Positive thought requires self-discipline, determination and personal choice. Mental stability contributes to the cycle of health for the physical body and for our spiritual well-being. An ability to feel value and significance in our lives allows us a sense of purpose and meaning. Spiritual health nourishes our interest in life. The nature of our thinking creates cycles of imbalance or balance in any or all areas of the mind, body and spirit. Balance is connected to embracing an enthusiastic perception of, and for, life.

Perception can affect or alter our reality within our physical environment. Five individuals experiencing the same event will interpret and retain different specifics of any given occurrence. So by changing our perception, we can create a different experience. Our thinking can either produce cycles of stagnant and repetitive behavioral patterns or enhance our personal and spiritual growth. If we continually indulge in undesirable thoughts about people, events and circumstances, our thinking will produce the experience of pain, suffering and misery. If we have a tendency to seek the positive in situations or events, even when they appear unbearably painful or challenging, we present ourselves an opportunity of acquiring strength and courage. We will also begin to feel balance, harmony and overall well-being.

The connection between our thinking and each aspect of the mind, body and spirit plays a significant role in our overall health and our perception of life. It is not what happens to us that causes pain and suffering or produces happiness and harmony. It is our thinking and understanding about our experiences that creates our reality and contributes to our overall health. What we believe in our minds is what we will experience in our reality. If we don't believe in something it will not exist.

Take control of your thoughts:

1. Catch yourself not being present or not paying attention to what you are doing at any given moment. When you observe that you are just going through the motion of an activity and you're absorbed in your thoughts, redirect yourself to the present moment. Never judge yourself or indulge in your thoughts. Allowing your mind to wandering away from the present moment can trigger unwanted emotions such as anxiety, boredom, insecurity, worrying or anxiousness about what is to come in the future.

2.   Don't evade feelings that surface. These feelings are ingrained emotional habits you have unconsciously conditioned yourself to automatically follow. Where there is no awareness there is unconsciousness. Bringing awareness to any feeling, behavior, action or thinking pattern is the first step to healing and change.

3.   Never attempt to suppress uncomfortable feelings. What we resist will persist. Allow your feelings without judgment, have total acceptance, and let them flow through you even if they are uncomfortable or painful. Painful or uncomfortable emotions will stay within your body unless you release them. The same emotions will continue to resurface through experiences your soul provides so you can heal that aspect of yourself. If you suppress your feelings, emotions will resurface more intensely, and eventually our bodies may develop a physical or emotional ailment. Releasing emotions means feeling them fully without judgment and with pure acceptance. They will eventually dissipate by allowing them to run their course and you will gain power over them.

4.   Listen to what your head is saying. Catch yourself not paying attention to your thoughts and redirect your attention to your internal dialog. Document what your mind rehearses through journaling. Notice any patterns of thinking when an emotional state arises. Awareness is the first step to change.

5. Attempt in every experience and circumstance to remain neutral. Neutrality keeps you from forming judgments and allows you to be open to absorb information without the mind's filtering process.

6. Ground or center yourself in your body. Grounding yourself is being present in any given moment. Being present allows you to stay neutral and keeps your energy centered within yourself. When caught up in the mind and emotions, you are releasing your valuable life force or energy to whatever or whoever is the focus.

Windows for Training the Mind—Sensory Focal-Point:

1. **Breath:** Bring air deeply into your lungs through your nose. Release air through your mouth. Keep redirecting if thought comes in. Continue until your mind is calm.
2. **Sight:** Focus on an object of interest (i.e. candles, mirror image of self, nature). Focus on the color, shape and size. Look up at the sky. Engaging your sight upward makes it difficult for your mind to wander.
3. **Smell:** Focus on the scent of plants, flowers, your home or the scent of food.
4. **Taste:** Focus on your taste buds when chewing gum, eating a meal or drinking liquid.
5. **Touch:** This includes physical exercise, artistic abilities, playing a musical instrument or hugging a loved one. Focus on the texture, temperature, and feelings within. Concentrate on your body's feelings and emotional energy.

6. **Hearing:** Concentrate on a sound. Sound can include music, crickets in the night or crackling of fire.

7. **Intuition:** Close your eyes and allow any images that appear. When your mind is in action, images are not from your intuition. Intuition manifests within the silence of a calm mind… an inner knowingness.

When your mind wanders, continually re-focus your attention and energy back on your preferred sensory focal-point. Do not become frustrated with your mind's continual babble. Stay centered and practice daily. Begin with one minute each day. Increase your focus time when you've stabilized a calm mind for one minute.

Indicators of the experience of a calm mind:
- Inner contentment or peace.
- Being present in any given moment.
- Colors and images appear enhanced.
- Life appears more vivid and deeply beautiful.
- Awareness of the mind's silence.
- Noticing the increased synchronicities within your life experience.
- Increased gratitude and reverence for all of life.
- An intuitional knowingness or understanding that can't be explained.

Remember that training the mind takes daily consistency, persistence and discipline. The commitment of self and mind mastery takes time and is never ending, however the results produce inner contentment and balance of overall health of the mind, body and spirit. The experience of a calm mind is difficult to articulate because the calm mind isn't a concept or a creation within the mind. It is an experience of consciousness, of being present in any given moment.

Chapter 3: The Mind's Effect on the Brain's Functioning

There is a difference between the mind and the brain. The mind's awareness can consciously or unconsciously affect the function of the brain. Attitude, thought and values modify the brain's function. Neurotransmitters are released through personal perspective that is formulated in the mind. Belief is nothing more than a formulation of conditioned thought. Neurotransmitter deficiency or imbalance influences our bodies by producing varied mental or physical diseases. The human body continuously reacts to emotions such as shame, pride, grief, frustration, anxiety, hurt, irritation and resentment as well as love, gratitude, acceptance, joy, compassion, altruism and courage. Mental and emotional struggles can produce energy chemicals that build inside a specific area of the body and eventually appear as symptoms of disease or imbalance. Emotional health triggers neurotransmitters that keep our mind and bodies healthy and in balance.

Deepak Chopra, in his book "The Book of Secrets" lists eight constant factors that arise repetitively in thought patterns and that affect the health of our body.

1. *Being anxious about the future*
2. *Reliving the past*
3. *Regretting old mistakes*
4. *Reliving yesterday*
5. *Anticipating tomorrow*
6. *Racing against the clock*
7. *Brooding over impermanence*
8. *Resisting change*

These factors tend to override efforts of finding inner contentment along with a calm mind state. They are conditioned thoughts developed over years of inner dialogue.

The mind's attitude, thoughts and values can alter the brain's functioning through changing perception. The various thinking states, emotions and behaviors trigger specific brain neurotransmitters to react. Different neurotransmitters produce different functions which effect specific parts of the body. The natural neurotransmitter chemicals are produced by information that is communicated between the body and brain. Our bodies listen to our mind and the brain produces the neurotransmitter as a result of thought.

It is estimated that 85% of Americans have some degree of neurotransmitter imbalance or deficiency. (1) Neurotransmitter imbalances include depression, sleep difficulties, fatigue, anxiousness, irritable bowel syndrome, fibromyalgia, hypertension, migraines, PMS and obesity. (1) Our bodies are continuously reacting to stress which produces negative emotions such as anxiety, hurt, grief, stress, frustration or resentment that are all a product of fear. These emotional stressors set up our bodies to continually respond in the "fight or flight" mode. This is not a natural state of the mind or body. The fight or flight response to stressors communicate to our body that we are facing direct danger. Our bodies aren't meant to be in this continual state of stress. Instead of being in harmony and balance, the body produces chemicals that put additional stress on the body and mind.

Neurotransmitters (2)

Neurotransmitter	Response	Mental Deficiencies	Site of Physical Deficiencies
Acetylcholine	**Emotional Stability** Motor behavior, Memory, Arousal, Learning, Mood, Sleep	Memory Loss	Muscle Spasms, Stomach, Spleen, Bladder, Liver, Sweat Glands, Blood Vessels, and Heart
Serotonin	**Emotional Stability** Reduces Aggression, Regulates Sensory Input, Regulates Sleep Cycle and Appetite Control	Irrational Emotions, Irritability, Sleep Disturbances and Hallucinations	Blood Clotting, Heart, Migraines and Stomach
GABA	**State of Calmness** Control Convulsions, Anxiety and Arousal. Keeps Brain Activity in Balance	Anxiety, Racing thoughts, Rapid heart, Insomnia, Constant "fight or flight", Panic	Central Nervous System
Epinephrine	**Adrenaline**	Stress, Anger, Fear, Fight or Flight Response	Increased Heart Rate, Metabolic Rate and Blood Pressure
Norpinephrine	**Motivation** Arousal, Energy, Drive, Stimulation, Fight or Flight, Lack of Energy and Motivation	Anxiety	Nervous System

Neurotransmitter	Response	Mental Deficiencies	Site of Physical Deficiencies
Dopamine	**Pleasure** Feelings of Pleasure, Attachment and Love. Sense of Altruism, Ability to Integrate Thinking with Feelings	Lack Pleasure, Remorse, Ability to Feel Love, Attachment Issues, Distractibility, Schizophrenia and Paranoia	Parkinson Disease, Depression, Restless Leg Syndrome, Tremors
Enkephalin	**Wellbeing** Internal Contentment, Sense of Wellbeing, Feelings of euphoria, Self-Understanding,	Aggression, Anxiety, Inner Turmoil	Lack of Pain Management, Physical Restlessness

Our man-made societal structure creates unnecessary life stressors. Our society has replicated an illusionary battlefield within the body and mind. Humans are meant to live in balance and harmony. Self and mind mastery allows you to maneuver through society with less stress or fewer pressures that are ultimately created by how we look at our circumstances and experiences.

Healing Through Change:

Changing something in your life is like learning to ride a unicycle. At age twelve, it took me one month practicing every day for several hours a day during a summer to learn to ride a unicycle. I never gave up and was determined to do it. Change is a process of reconditioning. It takes persistence, discipline and determination.

Change can be extremely difficult for many, however with change we allow ourselves an opportunity for personal and spiritual growth and development. Successful change is a rite of passage to higher levels of consciousness or energy frequencies. Through the change process, be sure to embrace without judging your current thinking, emotions and behavior. Awareness and acceptance of the self is what allows change to happen.

Every time you make a positive change in your life, you raise your consciousness vibration. You become a different person, a new person. You are no longer who you were before, so forgive any wrong doings or things you might have regret, guilt or shame for. These are things that no longer serve who you are becoming. These things or actions are no longer who you are presently. You are creating a new you. You are becoming the master of yourself.

Awareness is the First Step to Change:

1. Awareness is the first step to healing destructive and unwanted thinking and behavioral patterns.
2. Healing begins to occur only when you take full responsibility and acceptance for your contribution to difficulties in your life.
3. Healing is a process, so don't expect immediate results. Give gratitude for even the smallest breakthrough.
4. Pinpoint and visualize daily a different response to a behavior, emotion or circumstance you desire to heal. Move into it with acceptance. Remind yourself that behavior comes out of emotion and emotion comes from thought.
5. Allow yourself to feel fully your emotions or feelings. Feelings

and emotions are energy. Do not judge them or attempt to suppress them. Allow them to flow through you so the energy can be released.

6. Your goal has to become a part of your lifestyle. Your new behavior must become a part of who you are. Commit to discipline and self-mastery.

7. There will always be a cost involved in a beneficial change. You must be willing to give up, if even temporarily, the people or things that will hold you back.

8. Healing can be extremely challenging, extremely difficult and can also leave us feeling alone. Be your own advocate. All beneficial change outweighs any cost.

9. With change, your energy frequency changes. You will begin to see changes in your circumstances and you will draw more people into your life with the same frequency you are holding.

10. The change process is for replacing old behaviors and thinking with new behaviors and thinking. Crowd out the old without judgment to bring in the new.

11. Eliminate blaming others or yourself. Claiming personal responsibility fuels the healing process and creates empowerment.

12. Relapse or setbacks are a part of the change process.

Relapse or Setback Prevention:

1. Planning for relapses allows you to anticipate strategies for coping with barriers, stresses or roadblocks that might set you back.

2. Surround yourself with people who encourage you

emotionally and support your goals. While going through the process of change, we sometimes have to temporarily remove individuals or things from our lives that hamper our growth.

3.   If you relapse or have a setback, don't engage in negative self-talk that promotes guilt, shame or punishment. Replace these negative thoughts with something encouraging even if you don't believe it. Find gratitude in other things that are going right in your life. Never give up!

4.   Keep a daily journal and observe patterns that set you backwards. Focus on these patterns and practice reconditioning through daily affirmations and gratitude for your current accomplishments. Remember one step back is two steps forward or maybe three or four.

5.   Find someone supportive you can be accountable to. Someone you can call if you feel you are struggling or feel you are in a rut. Remember this person should not be a source of venting negativity. Have compassion for yourself and express your feelings with a pure heart and acceptance to what is.

STEPS to Behavior Modification Setting Personal Goals	EXAMPLE
Identify a specific behavior you wish to change (i.e. be more patient, healthier thoughts, better nutrition, maintain a cleaner home environment, less impulsiveness.)	**END GOAL:** I would like to let go of experiences once they are over. My mind tends to replay the event over and over.
Maintain a journal of your current thoughts and behavior (i.e. what behaviors or thoughts are you currently doing that contribute to the unwanted behavior?) There may be several behavioral factors involved.	**CONTRIBUTING THOUGHTS & BEHAVIOR:** I start replaying the event and imagine what I should have done or said. I replay how I could have reacted differently and imagine a different outcome.
Journal for one week the thoughts that contribute to unwanted behavior. Include feelings and what you are thinking.	**BEHAVIOR RISK:** I tend to place blame on external causes instead of taking responsibility for my contribution through my thinking and emotions.
Analyze the current behavior and plan your behavior modification. Plan appropriately to meet your needs and interests. Important: Replace one behavior with another.	**BEHAVIOR REPLACEMENT:** Every time I start to think about my experience, I will stop by focusing on breathing deeply to let go of my thoughts. I will redirect my thinking with a positive affirmation.
Develop a contract with yourself based on a specific goal and steps needed to achieve your goal. Add daily affirmations.	**GOAL:** I will gain control of my negative thinking. "I have control over my thoughts", "I have control over my feelings", "I am the driver of my mind".
Journal each time you successfully achieve your specified goal. Include your feelings and thoughts about your accomplishment and schedule rewards with anything you enjoy doing to reinforce the new behavior.	**Journal:** Each time I redirect my thinking I will treat myself to either a movie, concert, healthy dinner or time with friends or family.

(1) Gero, Glenn B., N.D.,D.Sc., R.H. (AHG), M.E.S., C.L.C. "Neurotransmitter Level
     Testing." *New Jersey*

         Holistic Health, NJ Alternative Medicine: Neurotransmitter Testing.

         N.p., n.d. Web. 10 Feb. 2015.

         <http://www.holisticnaturopath.com/neurotrans.htm>.

         college.com/wadsworth/session/1/397/56712780/19!xrn_18_0_A885
         8'
(2) King, M. *Medical Biochemistry Neurotransmitters - Human Physiology*
     (p.209). Retrieved

         July 12, 2005 from the World Wide Web:

         http://web.indstate.edu/thcme/mwking/nerves.html

Chapter 4: The Mind's Effect on Stress and Aging

"Nature giving you the face you have at twenty; it is up to you to merit the face you have at fifty." ~ Coco Chanel

Research has estimated stress to be a factor in over 90% of all illnesses. [1] Neuroscience has discovered "neuroplasticity" in which the brain continually changes as a result of our experiences. [2] Our thoughts influence every cell in our bodies. Through his studies, Deepak Chopra addresses the hundreds of research findings that verify how the aging process is much more dependent on individual beliefs and thinking. The way in which a stressful environment or circumstance is interpreted determines what fuels the brain's neurotransmitters into action. People can become healthier, happier and more successful by striving for optimism even when besieged in stressful situations. The ability to see things in a positive light not only diverts mental and physical illness, but also creates quality of life as we age.

There is a direct relationship between emotional dysfunction and its natural consequence to the physical body. An optimistic outlook on aging extends life by seven and half years even after taking into account factors such as age, gender, socioeconomic status, functional health, self-reported health and loneliness. [3] Self-perception has an overall effect on health and aging. Individuals with positive self-perceptions on aging demonstrate significantly longer survival than those who interpret negative self-perceptions of aging. Studies have found optimistic viewpoints create better health and longer life span, advanced achievements in exercise, higher employment performance and inner contentment. (4)   Simply believing that aging is inevitable and comes with a deteriorating body will fulfill your expectations.   Overall, a pessimistic self-perception of aging can diminish life expectancy by accelerating the aging process and optimistic self-perception can prolong life expectancy and slow physical aging.

To live a youthful existence at any age, you must reverse any harmful thoughts you have about aging. Many people think once they hit a certain age they are over the hill and their bodies will inevitably begin to decline. These beliefs will become a self-fulfilling prophecy. Thoughts are energy and with focus we will create what we believe in our reality. Aging can be slowed by intentional thoughts of youth, living fully in your body and being in the present moment.

The Most Beneficial Anti-Aging Habits:

Aging is a natural process. However there are several ways to slow it down. Most people are informed that these actions contribute to graceful aging, but many don't participate in them for the long-term benefits.

STRESS: We can see first-hand how stress affects aging by just looking at someone who has had an extremely challenging life. It is important to note that there are people who have lived unimaginably challenging lives and have aged gracefully. The difference is each individual's inner dialogue. Many times people who view external forces to be the problem and blame others for their emotions live in stress. Especially under challenging circumstances, stressful thoughts are created in the mind. We have a choice in our perception and by changing our thinking we can change our perception and simultaneously change our realty.

When feeling stressed, take several deep breaths and notice what your mind is saying. Are you feeling agitated because of what someone said? Are you upset because someone didn't do what they were supposed to? In any given stressful situation once you find the thoughts that fuel the emotions of stress, change the thoughts to something functional. "I am in control of my emotions"; "No one can make me feel anything I don't choose"; "I am patient and it is not necessary for me to feel stress because of someone else's irresponsibility". Changing your thoughts will change your perception and ultimately reduce stress from the experience. This is a practice that will take time for some because emotional reaction comes from a lifetime of conditioning. Awareness that you have control over your thoughts and emotions is the first step to changing them.

PHYSICAL EXERCISE: Physical exercise is key to keeping a healthy, strong body as we age. Exercise builds muscle, heart health and detoxifies your body through sweating. It releases the "feel good" endorphins and enhances self-confidence. You don't need long cardiovascular exercise. You can choose an intense twenty minutes every other day routine. Burst training is the fastest and most effective exercise to lose fat and build muscle. Burst training is short and rapid cardio sessions that support fat loss and muscle toning more vigorously than jogging or other cardiovascular exercise. This doesn't mean you should give up jogging or cardiovascular exercise if you enjoy them. If what you are currently doing works for you, continue. You can find hundreds of examples of burst training or your choice of exercise on

YouTube. For those who just have not found an enjoyable exercise, GET UP AND MOVE. Walk or bike instead of drive. Take the steps instead of the elevator. Anytime you have a chance to move your body do so and include thoughts of youthfulness.

Always choose a form of exercise you enjoy. If you dislike exercising you will bring that energy of dislike and create a self-defeating experience. It would be unfair to state you dislike all movement because our bodies aren't meant to be stationary all day. Our bodies, organs and brain love movement. We were built to move and keep active to stay healthy. With all the technology and entertainment society provides our minds have become numb and our bodies stationary.

Notice the difference between dislike and lack of motivation. Ask yourself: the last time you worked out how did you feel emotionally and mentally in your body? How did you feel about your accomplished workout? Dislike has a negative energy behind it. Motivation takes discipline. Just do it without thinking about doing it. Once you allow your mind to get involved, it will drown out your motivation.

- Every fifteen minutes get up and move for one minute or more even at your place of employment.
- If you are a television watcher stretch while watching. Do three reps of five to ten pushups every fifteen minutes or do some muscle building reps with weights. Add some squat reps. Just move every 15 minutes.

- If you have stairs in your home a good source of burst training is to do three to five reps of laps up and down the stairs. Between reps take two minutes. Start where you can even if it is only one lap.

NUTRITION: Nutrition is another key component to graceful aging. Daily antioxidants, vitamins, healthy fats and minerals are a necessity in maintaining health. With all the illness and the declining health condition of human beings over the past few decades, it is logical to link the decline in health and increase in disease to unhealthy lifestyles. Our food has become nutritionally dead and the majority of our body care and household products are laced with chemicals. Anything we put on our bodies is immediately absorbed into our blood stream. It is also important to note that cancer feeds off sugar and the majority of processed foods contain high fructose corn syrup or other refined sugars. Sugar also has been linked to the obesity epidemic in the United States. GMOs, processed foods, sugar, pesticides and chemicals are in almost all of our pantries and household products as well as in the air and water.

Our bodies are miraculous vessels with built in immune systems that are far more powerful than any man made synthetic and chemical pharmaceutical. We get sick because of what is put into and on our bodies. Disease, brain fog, fatigue, and even lack of motivation have all been linked to a nutritionally deplete diet. [5] Clean up your diet and you will be amazed at the results. What you eat is even more important than exercise. A healthy diet is what aids weight loss. Exercise builds strength and endurance. Both create a healthy youthful body and mind.

Simple Healthy Household Changes:

- Start making time to prepare healthy home cooked meals.
- Buy organic when possible. This includes yogurt, butter and milk.
- Push out bad eating habits by adding more healthy foods into your diet.
- For each non-vegetable serving on your plate, eat an equal portion of vegetables.
- Get in the habit of eating your vegetables first.
- Grab the whole fruit instead of the fruit juice. Fruit has a higher fiber content and will make you feel fuller. Many fruit juices are loaded with additional sugars.
- Use baking soda and vinegar as cleaning agents. They are less expensive and will not harm your health. Vinegar kills bacteria, mold and germs and baking soda is a deodorizer and scrubbing agent.

Toxins are harmful to our bodies, however stress and nutritional deficiencies are the root cause of most chronic disease. [6] Maintaining body and mind health throughout a life time, diet and nutrition are key.

Natural Foods sourced with anti-oxidants that protect cells from damage are key to gracefully aging. They include:

- Organic Teas
- Herbs
- Omega-3 Foods
- Organic Vegetables

- Berries
- Nuts
- Coconut Oil
- Essential Oils

What we put in our bodies is essential for good health. The highly processed, chemically based food industry produces nutritionally "dead food" that contributes to accelerating the aging process. Our bodies need nutrients to perform at the highest level. If we feed our body sludge, our bodies will feel like sludge and exhibit low energy, no energy or symptoms of disease. Plant based earth foods fuel our bodies with vibrant, healing and living energy. If we are eating processed foods filled with chemical preservatives our bodies will not sustain.

Avoid these age accelerating and disease promoting foods:

- Refined Sugar or Artificial Sugars
- Sugary Drinks
- Processed Foods
- Genetically Modified Organisms (GMO)s
- Trans Fats
- Carbohydrates

WATER: There are many benefits to drinking water. It is a natural substance for eliminating toxins through urination and transports nutrients and oxygen into cells. Consuming water reduces food cravings, raises metabolism, prevents constipation and is essential to our digestive health. Water keeps muscles and joints lubricated and elastic, boosts the immune system to help fight the colds, flu, as well as cancer and other common diseases. With our brains being 85% water, drinking more water helps us think with more focused clarity and concentration. It makes us more alert, boosts energy levels and is a natural remedy for headaches.

Drink more Filtered Water:

- Drink a 16 oz. (2 cups) glass upon waking to help flush toxins from the body and aid digestive health.
- Squeeze in fresh lemon. Lemon not only aids in weight loss, but also cleans the liver, cleans the bowels and alkalizes the body.
- Drinking 16 oz. (2 cups) of water 20 minutes before each meal helps aid in weight loss by making you feel fuller. It also aids in breaking down your food so your body can absorb the nutrients.
- Carry a water bottle and calculate 0.55 X your weight to determine how many ounces you should be drinking each day.

SLEEP: Sleep is so significant to our health. Lack of sleep can increase anxiety, add intolerance to stressful situations and impair problem solving skills. Lack of sleep also weakens proper body function. The more sleep we get, the clearer our mind will be and the greater our feeling of enhanced wellbeing. While it may not always be practical especially with young children, it is important to aim for at least 8 hours a night. Start a relaxing evening ritual to help prepare your body and mind for a good night sleep. Avoid falling asleep with electronic devices in your room and better yet, remove them from your bedroom altogether. Glows and electric and magnetic fields (EMFs) from these devices can disrupt your sleep pattern. Your room should be in complete darkness with a comfortable room temperature.

For those who don't get a good night sleep and even for those who do, napping provides many health benefits as well. It not only improves our ability to retain information, increases alertness, enhances creativity and heightens our senses. Our mind and body rejuvenate while we sleep. Set an alarm because napping for more than 30 minutes can make your head feel clouded and your body heavy.

Stress related racing thoughts can disrupt sleep. An effective way to calm the mind is through focusing on your breath. As thoughts race in, return to the breath focus.

Diminish Stressors and Worries Before Sleep:

- Start a night time journal releasing all your worries, anxieties and challenges from the day. Stay neutral without judgment while journaling. Add some gratitude affirmations at the end.
- Limit your caffeine intake. Do not consume any caffeine after 2 pm.
- For some people consuming alcohol before bed wakes them and disrupts deep sleep.
- Schedule an hour of reading from a book before bedtime. Not only will you become relaxed, it just might lull you to sleep.
- Meditation before bed not only calms your mind, but it relaxes your body.
- Listen to relaxing music before bed.

- Spray (pure) lavender oil on your pillow. Lavender's scent is known for aiding insomnia and easing anxiety.
- Exercising during the day helps aid a good night sleep.
- Take a warm bath and add lavender, lemon or peppermint essence oils with Epsom salts. These essential oils aid in relaxation, dispelling anxiety and encouraging sleep. Epsom salt's beneficial properties include soothing pain, relieving muscle aches, relaxing the body and easing stress. During your bath include relaxing music or read a book.

ESSENTIAL OILS: Essential oils are another gift earth provides for anti-aging and de-stress remedies. While oils can be pricey it is important to only purchase organic certified pure oils. Those with skin sensitivities should test for allergic reactions and those on medications should consult their doctor to make sure they won't have an adverse reaction to the medication. It is important to research each individual oil for proper use and proper testing for skin sensitivities or allergic reactions.

1. Frankincense has anti-aging properties, helps boost the immune system, reduces stress, promotes the regeneration of healthy cells as well as many other health benefits.
2. Lavender's youth promoter helps induce sleep and rejuvenates skin cells.
3. Myrrh helps maintain healthy skin, has powerful antioxidants and improves blood flow.
4. Sandalwood also has anti-inflammatory properties as well as skin softening, toning and astringent properties.

5. Geranium reduces the appearance of wrinkles, rejuvenates, balances and evens skin tone.

6. Clary Sage is known to smooth fine lines and wrinkles and balances the production of skin oils.

7. Sea Buckthorn protects skin from free radicals and is known to nourish and rejuvenate the skin. It also slows facial wrinkles.

Anti-aging Recipe for the Face and Neck:

- Frankincense 10 drops
- Geranium 6 drops
- Clary Sage 6 drops
- Myrrh 4 drops
- Sea Buckthorn Seed Oil 4 drops
- 1 Teaspoon organic sunflower oil or coconut oil
- 1 Teaspoon organic rosehip seed oil
- 1 Teaspoon organic witch hazel

Mix in an essential oil, small, brown or blue glass spray bottle.

(1) "ISTPP: The Congressional Prevention Coalition." *ISTPP: The Congressional Prevention Coalition*. N.p., n.d. Web. 10 Feb. 2015. <http://istpp.org/coalition/stress_prevention.html>.

(2) Goleman, Daniel. *Destructive Emotions: How Can We Overcome Them?: A Scientific Dialogue with the Dalai Lama*. New York: Bantam, 2003. Print.

(3) "Thinking Positively About Aging Extends Life More than Exercise and Not Smoking." *Yale News*. N.p., 29 July 2002. Web. 10 Feb. 2015. <http://news.yale.edu/2002/07/29/thinking-positively-about-aging-extends-life-more-exercise-and-not-smoking>.

(4) NewsRX. "Thinking Positively About Aging Extends Life More than Exercise

and Not Smoking." *Yale News*. Stanislav Kasi/Martin Slade/Suzannie Kunkel, 29 July 2002. Web. 02 Feb. 2015. <http://news.yale.edu/2002/07/29/thinking-positively-about-aging-extends-life-more-exercise-and-not-smoking>.

(5) Blake, Kati. "Nutritional Deficiencies (Malnutrition)." *Healthline*. George

Krucik, MD, 26 July 2012. Web. 12 Feb. 2015.

<http://www.healthline.com/health/malnutrition#Symptoms4>.

(6) "Don't Believe Everything You Think." *Stress Free Now*. Cleveland Clinic of

Wellness, n.d. Web. 10 Feb. 2015.

<http://www.clevelandclinicwellness.com/programs/NewSFN/pag

es/default.aspx?Lesson=3&Topic=2&UserId=00000000-0000-0000-

0000-000000000705>.

Chapter 5: The Mind's Effect on Emotional and Mental Ailments

"Wherever thought goes, a chemical goes with it; distressed mental states get converted into the biochemicals that create disease."

~ Deepak Chopra

Many people walk through day to day life in a clouded sense of perception and lack of awareness about the power of the human mind. Using the mind as a tool for creating life experiences is fundamentally more functional than using the mind as a dwelling place for the formulation of inaccurate belief systems and distorted view of the individual self. Mental illness is certainly one of the major health problems today. Eckhart Tolle, the author of The Power of Now, describes consciousness (awareness of the mind), as the spiritual aspect of the "self". He explains how human beings have an innate ability to "watch" the "thinker". The "I or consciousness" of an individual can notice what the "mind or ego" is creating, assuming and judging. (2) The ability to keenly "observe" the mind ultimately indicates two aspects of an individual: the spiritual nature (the "I" or "Awareness/Consciousness"), and the self (the "mind" or "ego"). (2) The ego is the formulation of a self-created persona developed through conditioning, hand-me-down beliefs and preference perception of life experiences. An individual's mind state also plays a significant role in circumstantial situations.

In Ageless Body Timeless Mind, Deepak Chopra, M.D., indicated that human beings are the only creatures on earth that can change their biology by changing what they think and feel. (3) Our cells react to our thoughts. Stressful circumstances, emotional upheaval or a phase of depression can inflict chaos and damage our immune system. Laughter and positive emotions such as love or compassion can boost our immune system. Our thoughts are energy and they communicate with the cells in our body. Balance or imbalance creates health or illness.

"Despair and hopelessness raise the risk of heart attacks and cancer, thereby shortening life; Joy and fulfillment keep one healthy and extend life; a remembered stress, which is only a wisp of thought, releases the same flood of destructive hormones as the stress itself."

~ Deepak Chopra

The nature of our thinking creates cycles of imbalance or balance in all areas of the mind, body, emotional functioning and life situations. Emotions manifest from thoughts and unpleasant thinking conditioned from childhood. Self-destructive beliefs and negative self-talk often go unchallenged and remain in the unconscious until awareness discovers it as false. Emotions often are misinterpreted as an individual's personality. Negative emotions of the personality are simply the human ego creating drama in the mind. You are not your mind. You are not your thoughts. Through the process of self-mastery you will experience who you really are outside of the mind chatter.

In the book The Creation of Health, Caroline Myss Ph.D. and Norm Shealy M.D. hypothesize that the majority of physical illness results from an overload of emotional, psychological and spiritual crises. (4) Their extensive study connects who we are, what we believe and how well our emotional needs are met within our environments and how it all contributes to health or disease. Our emotional states and mental attitudes influence our bodies tremendously and this manifests through either imbalance or wellbeing. Through our inner dialogue and perception preference we can transform our biology over time.

Myss and Shealy have identified eight dysfunctional patterns that have been shown consistently with people who become mental or physically ill. These include:

1. Unresolved or deeply consuming emotional, psychological or spiritual stress.
2. The degree of control that negative belief patterns have upon a personal reality.
3. Individual's inability to give or receive love.
4. Lack of humor.
5. The inability to distinguish serious concerns from the lesser issues of life.
6. How effectively one exercises the power of choice in terms of holding control over the movement and activities of their life.
7. How well a person has attended to the needs of the physical body; individual perception of purpose or meaning in one's life.
8. The tendency toward denial of what's not working in one's life. (4)

Human beings in their pure essence are not meant to be living in the mind or ego. Many people associate their thinking with who they are. However we are not our mind. The mind is a lifelong consolidation of experiences and inner dialogue that was invented by self-perception - our ego. This is proven by the fact that individual thoughts can be reconditioned, and through reconditioning, perception and emotion is changed.

Moving Through Emotion:

1. **Recognize**—that your thoughts create your emotions.
2. **Accept**—that you have control over your thinking.
3. **Choose**—to redirect your thinking by pausing and focusing on your breath.
4. **Decide**—to be in control of your emotions and not have your emotions in control of you.
5. **Learn**—not to allow yourself to react to stressors that affect your body, emotions, self-esteem, or values... be authentic.
6. **Acquire**—ownership of your thinking.
7. **Control**—your thinking and make a list of calming thoughts to remember (i.e. I'm in control, I can handle this, I'm safe, It's okay).

When in an emotional state, whether positive or negative, focus on the feelings within your body. Notice what your internal dialog is saying and ask yourself if it is a conditioned response. Focus deeply on feelings and allow them to enter your awareness. Resisting feelings only pushes them into dormancy. Repressed feelings will continue to resurface with more intensity or manifest as physical ailments or emotional instability. Repressed feelings can also resurface in uncontrollable anger or other negative emotions.

Notice what internal body energies you are feeling such as a racing heart, flushed face and ears, uncomfortable stomach, anxiety or headache. Internal emotions begin with thought. Thought transforms into emotion and emotion often fuels behavior. Eventually whether intentioned or not, self-dialog manifests health or imbalance in the body.

Learn About Your Emotion Triggers:

- Journal to identify irrational thoughts and statements that fuel emotions.
- Express the underlying emotions (fear, sadness, confusion, hurt) behind your feelings.
- Explore what the intention is behind the behavior or self-dialog you desire to change. Finding what the intention is will give it less strength and will open the door for new and healthier behaviors and thinking. Example: "When I become emotional and exhibit tears, people around me give me attention and I feel cared about and loved", "My sarcasm toward others makes me feel empowered", "I manipulate others because it makes me feel cleaver and smart." Whatever it may be there is always an underlying reason for conditioned behaviors to resurface over and over.
- Challenge self-destructive thoughts and recondition them with new calming thoughts.
- Stay internally calm when others try to push your buttons. Focus on your breath.
- Take a timeout when emotions flare during an argument or disagreement. After becoming calm return to solve the problem.

- Distinguish between little and big deals. If it is not that important to you, let it go.
- Identify old unresolved childhood issues that may be brought into current emotional triggers.
- Stop blaming others for your stress that is produced by your thoughts about an experience or circumstance.
- Observe and identify body reactions, emotions and thoughts during a perceived threat.
- Practice forgiveness—to forgive means to refuse to carry painful and debilitating grudges, shame, resentment, regret or anger around with you for the rest of your life. Forgiveness isn't saying what was done to you or another is OK. Forgiveness is acceptance of what is. It is letting go of the past. Forgiveness allows you to take back your power. Forgiveness removes the dense and heavy energy in your mind and body.

There is a deep interrelatedness between our state of consciousness and external reality. Awareness is always the first step to making personal changes.

(1) Myss, Caroline M., and C. Norman Shealy. *The Creation of Health: The Emotional,*
Psychological, and Spiritual Responses That Promote Health and Healing. New
York: Three Rivers, 1998. Print.
(2) Tolle, Eckhart. *The Power of Now: A Guide to Spiritual Enlightenment.* Novato, CA: New World Library, 1999. Print.
(3) Chopra, Deepak. *Ageless Body, Timeless Mind: The Quantum Alternative to Growing Old.* New York: Harmony, 1993. Print.
(4) Myss, Caroline M., and C. Norman Shealy. *The Creation of Health: The Emotional,*

Psychological, and Spiritual Responses That Promote Health and Healing. New

York: Three Rivers, 1998. Print.

Chapter 6: Meditation Effect on the Mind

"Self-discipline, or self-control, means taking possession of your own mind." ~ Napoleon Hill

Meditation is a tool for training the mind and altering states of consciousness. Meditation has proved itself as contributing to physiological and psychological well-being. It is the pathway to bringing the mind to a calm state. A calm mind is a level of consciousness that promotes healing. A calm mind creates an internal stillness of inner contentment. Meditation allows us to detach from thoughts, feelings, emotions or past experiences. It allows us to observe our thoughts instead of engaging in them. Observation gives us control over our thoughts. Engagement allows our mind to have control.

Some of the scientifically proven benefits of meditation include:
- Decreased metabolic rate.
- Lower heart rate.
- Lowered levels of chemicals associated with stress.
- Reduction of molecules that cause tissue damage.
- Decreased high blood pressure.
- Skin resistance.
- Drop in cholesterol levels.
- Improved air flow to the lungs. (1)

Meditation can increase brain wave coherence, decrease depression and anxiety, improve memory, increase emotional stability, mend addictions and improve powers of concentration. (2) Meditation also balances the right and left hemispheres of the brain.

It helps shift change and effort towards personal growth and development. Through meditation you can reverse the need for most medication through your innate power to heal your own body and mind.

Starting at birth, our minds are trained through conditioning. We can also re-train our mind through conditioning by observing and questioning our beliefs. Individual happiness and inner contentment can be enhanced through training the mind. The University of Wisconsin, Madison laboratory tested brain activity in one hundred and seventy five individuals and one Buddhist monk practitioner and scholar. Electrodes were placed on their heads and brain activity was measured in the region associated with strong positive emotion – the amygdala. Comparing results, the monk had the most extreme positive value out of the entire hundred and seventy-five subjects tested. (2) Consciousness is a transformation of the brain and awareness of the mind. Consciousness allows the personality to endure with more alertness, creativity and inner contentment.

Individual consciousness is essential for a paradigm shift within the collective of families, cultures, religions and society as a whole. Creating a disciplined balance within ourselves is the very means of accessing overall health and changing the world around us. Awareness is the initial means to the progression of change. Lack of awareness is both a condition and process based on the cause and effect of generational conditioning. Consciousness removes barriers and obstacles from those functioning without adequate external resources.

The elements of our environment and emotional existence either allow mobility of personal progression or suppress us into a dormant state of being. Constant thought within the mind shifts us from using our internal resources. These resources have become dormant through conditioned belief systems. These internal resources play an enormous role as to whether we attain inner well-being or become trapped within a cycle of repeated mental dialogue, consuming emotional and psychological distress or unpleasant re-occurring life circumstances.

Meditation is a practice that allows for composure of the mind, stress reduction and healing imbalances within the human energy field. It is an experience of shutting off the mind or detachment from thoughts.

Meditation for Beginners:

- Meditation is a form of internalization or focus within yourself. It is important to stay grounded within your body while meditating. Grounding keeps your energy within you. When you focus on an outside source you are giving your soul energy away.
- Sit in front of a mirror, focus on another object or sit quietly with your eyes closed. This can be on a chair, on the floor or any comfortable location.
- Make sure there are no distractions for the time period you will be meditating.
- Light a candle or incense in a dim room and hold the energy of grounding, compassion and love.
- Begin by focusing on your breath. Breathe deeply into your lungs through your nose, hold for two seconds and release from

your mouth. If thought sneaks in, just notice it and allow it to be. Refocus your attention once again on your breathing.

- Don't allow yourself to become frustrated when thought enters. Notice your thoughts with gratitude and continue to refocus on your breathing. Once you have mastered a minute without thought, increase your time slowly to a minimum of 10 minutes per day.

- Start practicing being present while doing activities. With presence, your mind isn't engaged in constant thought. Being present is another form of meditation and allows for the free flow of insights, understandings and intuition.

You can practice being aware of your thoughts in any situation by watching them instead of engaging with them. Eventually you will become the controller of your thinking. Your mind will no longer have control over you. This practice will allow you to reconnect to a stable vibration when there is disharmony around you.

Meditation Benefits:

- Greater connection with your soul or inner self.
- Increased access to your unconscious internal resources intuition, imagination and creativity.
- Improved management of thinking, emotions and behavior.
- Increased open-mindedness with a sense of direction and purpose in life.
- Improved ability to make sound decisions based on integrity and values.
- Increased inner contentment and passion for life.

- Increased perspectives for finding solutions to problems or road blocks.
- Increased ability to release negative emotions.
- Increased love and cooperation in relationships.
- Improved health, energy, vibrancy and mental focus.

With self-mastery you have no desire to control, manipulate or harm another. You find full acceptance in who someone chooses to be. You step aside from self-judgment or judgment of others. You feel alive with a compassionate loving heart. You can more clearly see the suffering, imbalance or wellbeing in others because you feel the energy behind their presence. When residing in the present moment, everything becomes available.

Training the mind takes daily consistency and determination. The commitment is enormous, however the results deliver an inner contentment and balance of overall health of the mind, body and spirit.

(1) Mayo Clinic Staff. "Meditation." : *Take a Stress-reduction Break Wherever You Are*. N.p., 19 July 2014. Web. 11 Feb. 2015. <http://www.mayoclinic.org/tests-procedures/meditation/in-depth/meditation/art-20045858>.

(2) Goleman, Daniel. *Destructive Emotions: How Can We Overcome Them?: A Scientific Dialogue with the Dalai Lama*. New York: Bantam, 2003. Print.

Chapter 7: The Mind's Effect on the Brain's Hemispheres

Eighty percent of what we take in from our environment is through our eyes. Each eye has dominance in either the right or left brain hemisphere. The brain's two hemispheres have unique functions and abilities. The two hemispheres communicate with each other by sharing information which creates our perception preference.

Our perception is evaluations and interpretations from what we hear, see and feel internally and externally. Our perception preference is created by the ego through experiences and conditioning. When living in the mind (ego), we often filter out specifics within the context of the whole of an experience. We only perceive what we believe and eliminate what we can't process based on our beliefs. These experiences make up our emotional composite and are absorbed in each hemisphere of the brain.

Left Hemisphere
- Logical
- Linear
- Analytical
- Data
- Facts
- Familiar Information
- Language
- Math & Science
- Computation
- Repetitive
- Organized
- Details

Right Hemisphere
- Spatial Information
- Metaphors
- Sense of Identity
- Emotions
- Unfamiliar Information
- Intuition
- Creativity
- Poetic Language
- Arts & Music
- Holistic
- Feelings
- Imaginatic

Most of us have a dominate eye which is paired to the opposite side of the brain. Left Hemisphere thinkers are more logical, objective and analytical, while right brain thinkers are more thoughtful, intuitive and creative. Both hemispheres capture what we hear, see and feel, but most of us have a dominate side. The Other Mind's Eye by Allen C. Sargent is based on research indicating human's ability to alter perception, solve problems, control thinking patterns, and increase internal awareness. Through the practice of accessing both hemispheres we have the ability to loosen consciousness dormancy. This is done by accessing the opposite dominate brain hemisphere through the practice of using the opposite internal eye. Each internal eye has distinctly separate encoded images of perceived experiences based on the hemisphere's functions and abilities. A major tool for creating personal change is the ability to retrieve internal images or create goals through visualization using both hemispheres.

The two hemispheres of the brain communicate with each other by sharing information. The separate hemisphere's function is to communicate between each other and combine into one perception. The transferring and sharing of information creates our experience with both hemispheres communicating their unique cognitive function. Within any experience, specific modalities (sensory channels) can be enhanced and program our brain to trigger a past positive or negative experience based on modalities within the current experience. Modalities include auditory, visual, tactile/kinesthetic, taste and smell.

With internal beliefs, even within a new experience, modalities can trigger past emotions or thoughts. Visual, auditory and kinesthetic are the three main sensory channels for processing information in the brain.

Three Main Processing Sensory Channels:

1. Visuals learn by seeing. They prefer reading text, pictures, film and diagrams to understand a concept. They remember faces and see images in their head. They prefer face to face contact. Visual learners remember with clarity colors, a movie or still picture or size and location.
2. Kinesthetic learners need a hands-on approach. They need movement and learn best with games, the internet or labs. They often use gestures and expressive movement and they get easily distracted by other activity. Kinesthetic learners remember through tactile, emotional evaluation, movement and spatial orientation.
3. Auditory learners respond well to discussion and lectures because they need to verbally hear something to absorb information. They prefer telephone communication over e-mail or text. They often become distracted by sounds and noises. Auditory learners remember through volume, location and content of words.

One way to know when an individual is processing in a specific hemisphere is through facial lateralization. At any given time a lifted mouth, eyebrow or face line on the left side of the face suggests right hemispheric dominance and the opposite holds true for the left hemisphere. (1) To gain internal control, it is important to practice shifting the perception to the other hemisphere. It is also important to note that whichever eye you look into while speaking to someone is going to have an influence on the other person's internal perception. (1) Directing your brain on purpose changes perception and loosens a mental and emotional dormancy.

Thoughts, emotions and behaviors can become like a tire rut in the mud. It becomes an indent, a form of being stuck in the repetitiveness. Shifting away from the dominate eye allows new knowledge and experience to enter awareness so that we can be our most resourceful self.

Practice Directing Your Brain between Hemispheres:

Shifting hemispheres loosens dissociation of painful memories and alters perception. Detachment or neutrality removes us from identifying with our emotions, beliefs and perceptions of a personal experience. Neutrality allows us to be the observer verses the actual participant in any given experience. To be associated to an event or situation merges personal perception preference which often times is filtered with belief, thought and emotion.

To gain internal control it is important to practice shifting your perception of any specific experience imprint to the opposite hemisphere. Directing your brain on purpose changes perception and loosens consciousness dormancy. It takes practice and flexibility to retrieve new information from the process of shifting between hemispheres.

1. Determine your dominate hemisphere by doing an internet search under "How to determine dominate brain hemisphere" and take a short test.
2. Once determining your dominate hemisphere, think of a challenging person or experience. Notice and write down each auditory, visual, tactile, taste and smell modalities. Shift your attention to other internal eye to retrieve unconscious information from the opposite hemisphere.
3. Notice any differences in modalities between the two hemispheres and pay attention to any shift in emotional response.
4. Determine which hemisphere you respond with more resourcefulness. The purpose is to retrieve unconscious or hidden information and to put knowledge and experience into awareness... changing perception.
5. Explore issues that may surface relating to self-defeating beliefs and dialogue, or negatively charged memories.
6. Practice shifting hemispheric dominance. Learning to access the other eye helps change perception and brings new awareness that we have life choices for changing circumstances, behaviors, beliefs and thinking patterns.
7. Follow up this process with exploring issues that may surface relating to limiting beliefs or negatively charged memories.

You can discover which hemisphere is dominant at any given time by noticing your thoughts and the seriousness (left brain) or emotional (right brain) of your attitude.

(1) Sargent, Allen C. *The Other Mind's Eye: The Gateway to the Hidden Treasures of Your Mind*. Malibu, CA: Success Design International Publications, 1999. Print.

Chapter 8: The Mind's Creation of Perception and Belief

"Whatever we plant in our subconscious mind and nourish with repetition and emotion will one day become a reality." ~ Earl Nightingale

Beliefs are a formulation of thought; a mind-created projection of the external things outside the individual self. Separation of mind and body from our spiritual aspect early in life results in eventual inner turmoil of fear, guilt, jealousy, shame and judgment. These emotions are then continually re-enforced through conditioned belief systems. The whole of our beliefs, thinking preferences and behaviors will contribute to our overall wellness or illness. Without the ability to calm the mind, we will live in the illusion of "being separate" from each other, nature and the universe. Ultimately, we become detached fragments of the whole.

Our mind state is strongly related to our mental, emotional and physical health. The problems we encounter when trapped in the monotony of life limited to our mind creations, distractions and distortions become inevitable pain and suffering. However, it is possible to make life-long changes for a more balanced and fulfilling reality.

Starting at birth, we are steered away from utilizing our internal resources, resources that tap into our higher self - intuition. Our lack of this awareness is often filled with seeking meaning in external projections whether it be, and not limited to, relationships, titles, education level or monetary value. Because of the way our society has been systematically created, we have lost our compass for reaching our innate and powerful internal resources... self-mastery.

Continually reaching to define our sense of self and inner contentment externally leads to a perpetuating cycle of meaninglessness, emotional restlessness or questioning life's purpose. Living life solely in the head removes the awareness of the minds power of creation. The human experience hasn't been based on each one of us being unique, but more so we experience being placed in categories or labeled.

Beliefs are based on what has been taught by family, friends, peers, religion and society. Individual beliefs are re-enforced through each reoccurring circumstance drawn by our belief system, in turn validated by our individual perception preference. **Reality can be altered simply by changing perception.** The attitude with which life is approached largely determines what we will see in people and what will be created in our reality. Those who have expectations or prejudgment about people, events or circumstances can effect another person's behavior or create a self-fulfilling prophecy through an experience. Prejudging people based on appearance or something we heard about them can alter someone else's normal attitude or behavior based on the energy we are projecting on to them. People also tend to project behaviors they unconsciously own onto others. Projection results in an unconscious influence of behavior or attitude that reinforces our perception as reality. Thinking preferences whether positive or negative will determine the level at which we will function in society. Individual circumstances are a mirror of our selective mind filter and inner dialog.

We will only see what we believe. If we do not believe in something, it will never manifest into our physical reality. Quantum physicists explain if something is not in our level of consciousness or belief system, we will not be able to process it as reality even though it exists. Based on our particular preference perception, our mind will filter out any information that does not pertain to our current held beliefs or level of consciousness. Five individuals experiencing the same event will interpret and retain different specifics of any given occurrence. By simply altering our individual interpretation of an event, our brain functioning changes and a different experience is created internally and externally.

Questioning beliefs can shake the entire foundation from which we as individuals derive our sense of self (the ego/mind). Not allowing new information to infiltrate our firmly held beliefs creates stagnancy and an internal dormancy of consciousness. **Being open to new information expands our awareness and allows us an opportunity for internal and circumstantial (external) change.**

To illustrate this point, Carl Sandburg related an allegory in his book, The People. It is a story about a 19th century Kansas pioneer.

"He leaned at the gatepost and studied the horizon and figured what corn might do next year and tried to calculate why God ever made the grasshopper and why two days of hot winds smother the life out of a stand of wheat and why there was such a spread between what he got for grain and the price quoted in Chicago and New York."

"Drove up a newcomer in a covered wagon:"

"*What kind of folks live around here?*"

"Well stranger, what kind of folks was there in the country you came from?

"Well, they was mostly a low-down, lying, thieving, gossiping, back-biting lot of people.

"Well, I guess, stranger, that's about the kind of folks you'll find around here."

And the dusty gray stranger had just about blended into the dusty gray cottonwoods in a clump on the horizon when another newcomer drove up:

"What kind of folks live around here?"

"Well, stranger, what kind of folks was there in the country you came from?"

"Well, they was mostly a decent, hard-working, law-abiding, friendly lot of people."

"Well, I guess, stranger, that's about the kind of folks you'll find around here."

We take with us the whole of us, where ever we go, be it a relocating, a vacation, a new relationship or changing employment. Our beliefs, thoughts and behaviors go along with us on these new journeys. If we are looking to create a new experience, we won't find it unless we release and change our perception of who we are.

The societal system of culture, religion and education feeds the ego. The system unplugs humans from our inherent nature and connection to the earth and soul energy. This energy is the connection to life itself. Our mind has been fed by culture, society, family, education, religion, media and politics. All of these divide us by pitting us against each other through categories, levels, labels and differences. Unintentionally, our mind gets caught up in the jumble of everything society and the media feeds it through propaganda and falsehoods. This separates people and re-enforces the mind away from the heart. The heart is where love resides and without this connection, all other emotions that are derived out of fear sneak in our day to day lives.

A human being is meant to "being" in the present moment. Labeling encourages the mind to exist in society and the mind encourages the system to survive. Freedom is an illusion within a societal structure. There is no freedom when we are enslaved in the head. Society removes the connection to nature, each other and the whole of existence. We have been led to believe we cannot monitor ourselves, which leads to the false belief that humans are faulty or flawed. This occurs only in a societal structure that promotes fear, differences and separation from the whole. Our true nature is love, compassion and consciousness. When connected to the soul we are connected to love and compassion for self, earth, nature, animals and people.

Beneficial Change is the Catalyst to Personal Growth and Development:

- Change allows you more strength, courage, and self-esteem.
- Change allows you a feeling of purpose and meaning.
- Change allows you to see how your behaviors impact others and how others interact with you.
- Change allows you to begin to move beyond your old negative patterns of behavior and thinking into more creative

and constructive beliefs about yourself and your life circumstances.

Focus on what you are grateful for in your life even if is as simple as a meal. Start your day with daily affirmations that encourage self-acceptance and optimistic thoughts.

Irrational Beliefs/Self Abandonment	Rational Thinking/Self-Acceptance
I unconditionally need love, respect, approval and validation from my family and friends.	Love, respect, approval, and validation are amazing, however they are not necessary for my survival or wellbeing. I love, approve, respect and validate myself.
I will avoid disapproval of any kind.	While disapproval can be unpleasant, it is not catastrophic, and I will survive. I approve of myself.
I can't stand when I make mistakes. Mistakes make me feel like a failure.	My mistakes are an opportunity to learn and grow. Mistakes are a great resource for me to know what not to do next time. There are no mistakes when living a conscious life.
I'm helpless. I am a victim. I'm worthless. I am not worthy.	I'm solely responsible for my thinking, choices and behavior. While bad things happen, I am strong and courageous to move through them. I accept myself unconditionally.
I am devastated when someone doesn't like me or misinterprets me.	I can't control what others think of me and accepting myself is more important than how others view me. I have value and worth.

Irrational Beliefs/Self Abandonment	Rational Thinking/Self-Acceptance
I'm tired of people upsetting me or making me angry.	I have complete control over how I perceive a situation. My feelings are solely my responsibility. I choose my feelings based on my thoughts. I have control.
People need to stop judging and condemning me.	I can't control or change other's thoughts, behavior or actions. I solely choose my emotions by my perception of any given situation. I am only harming myself by getting upset about external forces I have no control over. I am in control.
My unhappiness is caused by things outside my control. There is nothing I can do when these external forces control my life.	External factors can be out of my control, but it is my thoughts about the external circumstances that cause my feelings and actions. I can learn to control my thoughts. I do have choices for what happens in my life.
If I don't worry about things that could go wrong, they might happen.	No news is good news. Worrying will not stop events from happening. Worrying will only create anxiety and discomfort.
I can be happier by avoiding life's difficulties, unpleasantness and responsibilities.	Avoidance is a short term solution and it creates unnecessary anxiety. Avoiding problems can make things worse at a later date. Immediate attention gets immediate results whether it is the outcome you desire or don't desire.
Events from my childhood are what cause my difficulties today. My experiences influence who I am today and I have no control over past hurts.	My past can't influence me anymore. My current beliefs cause my reactions and feelings. I may have learned these conditioned beliefs from my past, however I am solely responsible to change them in the present. I will use

Irrational Beliefs/Self Abandonment	Rational Thinking/Self-Acceptance
	my past experiences as an opportunity of acquiring strength and courage.

Noticing your thoughts is the first step to changing unwanted beliefs. Practice replacing pessimistic thinking with optimistic thoughts. At every opportunity, recondition any negative thought with an affirmation of inner contentment. Even if you don't believe the replacement thought or affirmation, keep saying it because eventually you will start to believe it through reconditioning old thought habits. Changing thinking patterns takes persistence and practice. The more you work at it the better you'll get. Remind yourself that you can't unlearn something that is brought into your awareness. Noticing old self destructive thinking and replacing thoughts with optimistic affirmations is the process of reconditioning. The new way of thinking will eventually stick.

Chapter 9: The Mind's Effect on Consciousness

"The key to growth is the introduction of higher dimensions of consciousness into our awareness." ~ Lao Tzu

The theory of Neuroscience explains that varied levels of awareness or consciousness control the brain's function. Buddhist theology explains that the evolution of human existence is to evolve beyond the mind; to live in a higher level of consciousness; to live in a state of presence that has no duality. This state is pure love consciousness. Without an acquired awareness and persistence, a reversal to unconsciousness cannot happen. With consciousness, personal responsibility becomes priority. Training the mind allows us to turn off the mind chatter. When the mind is used only as a tool, the experience of living in the present moment eliminates duality and karma of the physical world. Life is no longer seen through clouded perceptions of the minds creations or the ego no longer leaps between emotional states. With the mind clear of thought, the illusions of the ego are revealed as something that was created by the self. With no thoughts and just presence, consciousness experiences everything being connected.

Consciousness can be raised to higher levels through being present or lowered when we allow ourselves to be swept away with negative emotion. The deeper the focus on the internal self through meditation or presence, the higher the level of consciousness grows. The silent mind is consciousness. Consciousness allows the personality to endure with more alertness, creativity and inner contentment. Being unconscious is merely living life in the mind and engaging in negative emotions such as judgment, jealousy, revengefulness, regret and shame. Being conscious is a state of awareness of the self, thoughts, actions and behaviors. With awareness of the internal self, your primary focus is on personal responsibility and self-care. With consciousness comes knowing that what you do or say about others is in turn harming or balancing yourself. Consciousness is knowing and deeply feeling the interconnectedness with all of life. Everything is made of energy and all energy intertwines and affects everything in and around it.

Consciousness is self-mastery of living in a state of love and compassion. Self-mastery is knowing how thoughts, feelings and mental images create individual reality. Creative visualization can change experiences and circumstances. **Changing thoughts and feelings change personal reality.** Always keep in mind intention. Be cautious with desires and how choices might affect others. Using the power of visualization (imagination) to harm others with destructive choices, actions or behaviors will eventually return to the maker. Nature always aspires to balance. If actions are beneficial to others, this influences our lives favorably. It is impossible to hide behind or fake an intention that is self-serving. Intention must be genuine and beneficial to life itself. If the motive behind an intention is only to fulfill a personal desire, the outcome will be based off that energy. The choices that we make, our behavior and our thoughts will return to the level at which we are aware of our actions. It is a universal law... a boomerang effect.

Consciousness is being in a loving and companionate state. The collective of human consciousness has been suppressed through society's systematically planned alteration of the human existence. "We" has become "Me" through conditioning and programing within our education, religion, culture, politics and beliefs. What society has set humans up for is an environment of entertainment, a state in which we don't think for ourselves or question what we are being fed. Entertainment moves us away from internalization. Constantly watching television for entertainment, believing what we are told without questioning its authenticity, not revisiting where our beliefs originated are all road blocks and are a detriment to self-discovery or self-mastery.

Being able to sit in silence with our self while enjoying our own company is part of self-mastery. It is initially difficult to sit with our self when self-dialogue and self-doubt sabotage our progress. Keeping busy through constant activities or being entertained by outside sources numb the mind instead of calming it. Calming the mind puts us in control of what thoughts we allow to enter. **We become the master of our thoughts instead of our thoughts mastering us.** A numb mind doesn't allow for self-discovery. It doesn't progress personal or spiritual growth. Our society is set up to provide entertainment so the system can continue without people questioning or participating in changing it. We need to become involved and contribute to a paradigm shift away from the material world and into a collective consciousness where we are all connected and everything that happens to a part of the whole will affect all of us. This includes nature, oceans, animals, ecosystems and the earth as a whole.

Acquire Self-Mastery Through Consciousness:

Consciousness begins with awareness of your feelings, actions and thoughts. If you are in a negative mind state or any adverse emotion, your energy level becomes denser, less conscious. Through engaging in a lower vibration through negativity we lose vital life energy. Negativity in any form separates us from our higher self, which is consciousness.

1. Bring joy into your life. Do more things that make you happy and excited to be alive. Surround yourself with people who support and encourage you. Remove those who intentionally belittle or criticize you. Once you master increasing your energy frequency, the actions of these individuals will no longer affect you personally. Others who are seeking inner-peace will recognize your own inner contentment and be drawn to your energy and you to theirs.

2. Self-awareness is the first step to change. Start a daily self-talk journal. Write down everything you say to yourself during a one-day period. Notice common themes in your thinking and write them down. Notice your emotions throughout the day and journal them as well.

3. Once you've journaled for an entire day, go back and read the journal and question where your thoughts and feeling originated. An example would be self-doubt. You were asked to do something at work and you had an immediate feeling of incompetence or fear. What were you thinking or what do you believe about yourself that created that feeling? Try to pinpoint the thought that created the emotion or feeling. If you can't pinpoint the thought, try to notice what outside

event or person agitated your choice feelings. If you can't figure out where the emotion comes from, most likely it is from a subconscious experience triggered through modalities (sensory channels). Meditate on finding the experience to pinpoint where the emotion originated.

Personal Outcome of Increased Energy Consciousness:
- The understanding that you have control over your circumstances and your life.
- The understanding that you have control over your thinking, emotions and behaviors.
- The sense of individual purpose and self-worth.
- A consistent flexibility to adapt to the challenges, stresses and opportunities that are presented in your life.
- The intuitional knowingness that there are no coincidences— only personal creations and universal synchronicities.
- The ability to create your life circumstances more freely.
- A clarity, acceptance and inner contentment.
- Complete acceptance of others without judgment.
- Release of the need to control the environment or others.
- The feeling of oneness with others and nature.

Increasing Consciousness or Energy Frequency:

- **Music:** Listen to uplifting music without vocals. Most of the heavy metal or hard rock music is at a denser vibration and can disturb a positive emotional state. Allow your feelings to access what is calming and uplifting versus what drags you to a lower frequency.

- **Meditation:** Sit in silence with yourself and notice the thoughts and feelings that enter. Do not become agitated if they are negative because that in itself will lower your frequency. Consciousness is awareness. Low energy consciousness is without focus on or attention to chosen behaviors or thoughts. Practice daily.

- **Nature:** Nature is a high frequency in the purest form. Take a walk in nature and be aware of what goes through your mind or what feelings surface. Notice the beauty around you and just be present. With presence the mind is calm and the three dimensional world becomes more vivid and alive. No negativity can enter the space of presence.

- **Presence:** With intention, live each and every day in the present moment. Even when you need to use your mind, be present in it. Release the past and stop waiting for the future. Notice when you are just going through the motion of daily rituals without conscious awareness.

- **Laugh and Smile More:** Surround yourself with people and things that make you smile and laugh. Laughter brings consciousness to light and negativity can't be in the same space. Smiling and laughter releases endorphins that increase happiness and simultaneously raises your energy frequency. Your brain doesn't know the difference between a fake or real smile. Force a smile for the brain interprets facial muscles. (1) Find humor in life experiences and learn to laugh at yourself.

- **Exercise:** Exercise releases the feel good neurotransmitters in your brain. Choose an exercise you enjoy so your focus stays in the positive. Be present in whatever activity you choose. Remember presence is conscious awareness without thought continuously running.

- **Gratitude and Affirmation Journal:** Start an affirmation and gratitude journal. Write down the gratitude you have taken from the day or the blessings in your life even if small. With conscious intention, put in writing optimistic affirmations that you'd like to appear in your life. Write them as if they are already happening.

- **Ask the Universe or God for Assistance:** Any assistance or question you have will be answered if you ask. Be watchful for answers for they can come through a person, a book, social media or in any means imaginable. Assistance comes in the form of synchronicities that appear in our lives.

People often define self-worth by material wealth, accomplishments or socioeconomic status. We often say "I am a mother, a wife, a business owner", etc. All of these are an illusion of who you really are. Ask yourself who you would be without using external factors to define yourself. What would happen to you if you lost any of the things you currently define yourself as? Who would you be? If you are in the present moment with a calm mind, who would you be?

Contemplate and journal on these questions without using any external factors within the answers.

1. Who am I?

2. How do I define myself?

3. What do I value in myself?

4. What are my most enduring qualities?

5. Do I feel all people have the same value?

6. What do I feel in my heart?

7. Am I a good person?

8. Am I a compassionate person?

(1) Gothard, Katalin, MD, PhD, Evan Carr, BS, Shih-pi Ku, PhD, and Sebastian

(2) Korb, PhD. "News Releases Archives." *Society for Neuroscience*. N.p., 14 Oct.
2012. Web. 10 Feb. 2015. <http://www.sfn.org/Press-Room/News-Release-
Archives/2012/New-Research-Reveals-More-About-How-the-Brain-
Processes-Facial-Expressions-and-Emotions?returnId=%7B0C16364F-DB22-
424A-849A-B7CF6FDCFE35%7D>.

Chapter 10: The Mind's Effect on Physiology

"I'm a big believer in what's called personalized medicine, which refers to customizing your health care to your specific needs based on your physiology, genetics, value system and unique conditions."

~ David Agus

The body and mind are dynamically interconnected and both directly influence each other. The human body contains hundreds of locations where there is focused and concentrated energy. Everything that goes on in our minds, every action we take and every behavior adds up and becomes an accumulation of energy within our bodies. We create every outcome within our wellbeing or imbalance based on our thoughts, action and behaviors. Our physical and mental wellbeing or disharmony is the outcome.

Our inherited genetics do not predispose us to specific family illnesses. We have more control over our health than we have been lead to believe by science and Western medicine. Our thoughts are energy and what we focus on will eventually manifest. Our inner dialog disperses energy throughout our body's cells. A mental or physical illness that continues to appear within a family's genetic history is based on lifestyle behaviors, thought patterns and emotions that have been passed down from generation to generation. Predisposition of genetics can be challenged and changed by altering our perception, changing our thoughts and beliefs, changing unhealthy lifestyle habits and holding a belief in the power to heal.

Quantum physics theory explains that everything is a vibration of energy. Thoughts are energy and they mold and create our personal reality. Modern physics has proven that everything around us is moving energy and nothing is solid. Even a rock is energy, however it is much denser than higher vibrations such as human beings or an animal. Science has also confirmed that all matter is energy and can be influenced by thought. In 1998, the Western Journal of Medicine published the works of a six month double blind study done on distant prayer (projected thoughts) for health of individuals with AIDS. Psychic healers from around the United States were recruited to pray for the health of patients with advanced AIDS. Neither the healers nor the patients were introduced. The extraordinary findings had shown that the group prayed for had significantly fewer stage-related illnesses, enhanced mood and fewer hospitalizations than did the control group. The results were so astonishing that the National Institutes of Health funded an additional $1.5 million for further research in this area. [1]

There are seven energy centers in the physical body called chakras. Each chakra is recognized as a focal point for life-force relating to spiritual, physical, emotional and mental energies. The state of each charka reflects the health of a particular area of the human body. It also reflects emotional, psychological and spiritual well-being. Every thought and experience in an individual's life gets filtered through the body's energy system and recorded into the cells and chakra databases. When emotional or physical illness arises, it is because the chakra energy related to that body area has been affected or blocked.

Chakra's Power Center (2)(5)

Chakra	Color, Location, Function	Physical Imbalances	Psychological Imbalances
7th or Crown	**Violet** Crown of head: Understanding, Spirituality **Imbalance:** Attachment	Baldness, Brain tumors, Cancer, Epilepsy, Migraine headaches, Parkinson's disease, Pituitary problems	Excessive gullibility, Memory disorders, Multiple personalities, Nightmares, Split personality
6th or third eye	**Indigo** Center of forehead: Intuition, Seeing, Wisdom **Imbalance:** Illusion	Brain tumors, Cancer, Central nervous system problems, Eye and visual problems, Headaches (sinus), Sinus problems	Extreme confusion, Fixations, Inability to focus, Intelligence deficiencies, Living in a fantasy world, Paranoia, Poor visual memory, Psychotic behavior, Schizophrenia, Severe retardation
5th or Throat	**Blue** Center of throat: Communication, Expression and creativity **Imbalance:** Dishonesty	Ear and hearing problems, Cancer, Lymphatic problems, Mouth problems, Neck and shoulder problems, Parathyroid problems, Speech problems, Teeth problems, Thyroid problems, Throat problems	Inability to express self in words, Logorrhea (nonstop verbal charter), Poor auditory memory, Stuttering
4th or Heart	**Green** Center of chest: Love	Auto-immune system problems, Circulatory problems, Heart problems, High blood pressure, Lung cancer, Lung problems,	At war with yourself, Feelings of alienation, inability to bond with another, Self-destructive tendencies, Suicide

Chakra	Color, Location, Function	Physical Imbalances	Psychological Imbalances
	Imbalance: Loss or Grief	Respiratory problems, Thymus problems, Upper back problems, Vascular problems	
3rd or Solar Plexus	**Yellow** Above the navel: Identity, Control, Power, Will, Assertiveness **Imbalance:** Shame	Absorption problems, Adrenal problems, Arthritis, Anorexia nervosa, Cancer, Coordination problems, Liver problems, Multiple sclerosis, Obesity, Premature aging, Stomach problems	Addictive personality, Catatonic schizophrenia, Compulsive behavior, Excessive anger or fear, Manic-depressive behavior, Obsessive behavior, Sleep problems
2nd or Sacral	**Orange** 2" below naval: Pleasure, Sexuality, Desire, Procreation, **Imbalance:** Guilt	Anemia, Allergies, Diabetes, Diarrhea, Duodenal ulcers, Hypoglycemia, Kidney problems, Leukemia, Lower back problems, Pancreas problems, premenstrual syndrome, Spleen problems	Chameleon personality, Depression, Hysteria, Unable to be sexually intimate
1st or Root	**Red** Base of spine: Family, Survival, Grounding **Imbalance:** Fear	Cancer, Colon problems, Bladder problems, Female reproductive-organ problems, Fluid retention, Male reproductive problems, Sciatica problems, Urethral problems, Yeast infection	Accident prone, Being in survival, Dependent personality, Identity crisis, Weak ego structure

(2)(5)

Most people believe disease is just poor luck passed down by genetics. Disease appears because of lifestyle choices, inability to cope the stressors in life, air, water and food pollution, pessimistic belief systems, unresolved feelings and negative internal dialog. Illness comes from being out of balance and wellness returns with inner balance. Homeopaths theorize that covering mental or physical symptoms with a medication or surgery only suppresses them and moves them deeper into the cells. Eventually these symptoms manifest into a more severe illness or psychological disorder. The key is to reverse the origin of illness whether it be thinking patterns, unhealthy eating, lack of body movement, stress or chemicals in the environment.

Clear Out Your Chakra Centers:

- Use the chart above to find symptoms you may be experiencing and determine which chakra center is affected or blocked.
- Determine the physical and psychological imbalance you are experiencing.
- Start exploring the psychological imbalance with intention and send healing thought energy to the chakra center of focus.
- Visualization is one of the most powerful tools for creating what you desire in your reality. Daily and with intention, visualize clearing all energy centers through universal healing energy, which is love.

- Meditate on clearing your energy centers and healing past hurts. Never try to suppress or run from emotions or feelings. Accept them fully without judgment. Allow them to just be.
- Open your heart chakra and bring love and compassion into every action, thought, or spoken words.
- Intention takes practice, persistence and focus. Our thoughts are energy in creation so nothing is more beneficial than healing and reversing detrimental self-talk.

Western Medicine has polarized our ability or our belief that we have the power to heal ourselves. Our bodies are miraculous vessels made with a built in immune system that is far more powerful than any synthetic manmade drug. Many doctors have made claims that they are not educated in medical school about the value of nutrition for human health or how powerful self-dialog, perception to life experiences and beliefs affect our bodies overall health or disharmony.

Since the industrial age, our society has lost connection with what creates health and balance within our mind and body. We have been led to believe chemicals and pesticide-laced foods won't harm us. Chemical cleaning products kill germs, however we don't consider what these chemicals are doing to our bodies. We are led to believe that pharmaceuticals are better for us than nature's pharmacy, our natural immunity and ability to heal. Years and years of abusing our mind and our body builds up and the ticking disease and aging clock slowly creeps in day by day.

Orthodox doctors are educated and trained to administer drugs and surgery for managing symptoms. There is no healing that occurs in the Western medicine approach when it comes to physical disease or mental health issues. Doctors are not trained in nutritional health for healing or prevention unless they re-educate themselves to a holistic approach called Functional Medicine. There is a place for Western medicine when it comes to emergencies such as an accident, a heart attack, emergency surgery or a broken bone. However, when it comes to physical and emotional health, administering drugs or surgery only covers up the underlying cause, which in most cases is lifestyle choice, diet, stress, and negative self-dialogue.

Functional Medicine looks at the whole of an individual to find the root cause of symptoms and aliments. It is basically an analysis of stress, unhealthy lifestyle choices, mindset, relationships and emotional health... anything to do with what is not in harmony in an individual's environment, mind, body or spirit. There is a paradigm shift occurring within the health care field. Limitations, exploitations and deceptions are moving doctors in the direction of the Functional Medicine approach.

"The good physician treats the disease; the great physician treats the patient who has the disease." ~ Sir William Osler

How and why we have gotten to the point of covering up symptoms with pharmaceuticals and surgery? It began in 1847 when the American Medical Association (AMA) was formed because of the economic competition between doctors and the popular homeopath and alternative medicine practices. Doctors began labeling homeopaths as quacks. Until the turn of the century alternative medicine and homeopath practices remained commonly accepted choice for healing. New and extremely cost-effective medical treatments began emerging and they were so profitable that the AMA gained financial backing from the Rockefellers and Carnegies. (3) These financial gurus helped transform medicine into the profitable billion dollar industry it is today. Nature can't be patented, so plant based medicine is not a profitable industry. The billion dollar Western medicine industry grew out of the booming patenting of synthetic chemical drugs and medical machines. Through the AMA, doctors changed licensing regulations and standards allowing only orthodox doctors to legally practice any type of medicine. These new regulations excluded homeopaths and other alternative medicine competition. Twenty years later the wealthy AMA dominated medical practice drove a propaganda media campaign associating homeopath medicine as unscientific and pure quackery.

There is a place for pharmaceuticals for disease and symptoms. However healing will not come from masking the root cause. Reversing symptoms is accomplished through changing lifestyle and diet. Prevention through a healthy lifestyle and mindset is key to health.

Just as the alternative medicine propaganda machine destroyed homeopaths as healers, industrial hemp and medical marijuana became illegal through main stream media propaganda. Industrial hemp is not a drug. Unlike its cousin marijuana, industrial hemp has low THC, the chemical that produces the high. Hemp and cannabis as a medical alternative is one of the safest therapeutically active substance known to man without the detrimental side effects that prescription drugs have.

Currently our civilization is consuming fossil fuels that represent hundreds of millions of years of carbon deposits. We are stripping the last remnant of our planet's protective mantel of old-growth forests, causing environmental destruction, desertification and serious changes to the world's climate. (6) Hemp was one of the first domesticated crops and has been as a superior alternative to the paper, oil, cotton, pharmaceutical and lumber industries. (6) Not only is it a plant from the earth but it is a very nutritious food that produces more protein, oil and fiber than any other plant on earth. Today Hemp can provide over 50,000 industrial uses including medicine, shampoo, soap, clothing, food, building supplies, paper, plastics and fuel. (4)

It is important to take charge of our own health and healing. Much of what we believe about our emotional and physical health is false. Clean up your environment, self-dialogue and your diet before disease and disharmony creeps in. If you are dealing with health problems, find a Functional Medicine doctor who will guide your healing process by exploring the root cause of illness and disease. Find a health coach to help you create a personalized "map to health and wellbeing" that is unified to your inimitable lifestyle, interests and health goals.

Clean Up Your Mental and Physical Health:

Our minds and bodies are constantly being bombarded with toxins in our food, water, air, homes and by taking prescription pharmaceuticals. Illness and the declining health condition of human beings over the past few decades has been due to an overload of unhealthy processed foods, pesticides and chemicals in almost all household products as well as air and water pollution. We are sick because of what we put in and on our bodies.

Clean up your Internal and External Environment:

1. If you need help to identify and achieve your goals and make changes to better your health and overall wellbeing, hire a health coach.

2. Take time to de-clutter your surroundings. Holding on to things you don't need or use creates dense energy. Get rid of all things you do not use or clothes you do not wear. Give these away to others or a charitable organization. Giving freely with an open heart will bring abundance back. Giving is the same as receiving. When you give with compassion, you receive gratitude for giving, creating a continual cycle of give, receive, give and receive.

3. Remove chemicals from your home and go all natural. Start with cleaning supplies and body products containing chemicals and replace them with all organic and non-toxic products. Vinegar and baking soda are great for most cleaning jobs. The non-chemical products work just as well and there will be no more toxic residue to inhale or absorb through the skin.

4. Find a mercury safe dentist and have your mercury amalgam fillings removed. There is no safe level for mercury in your body.

5. Meditation provides healing to the body and mind as well as reduces stress. Make it a daily practice and focus with the

intention to heal aspects of yourself that are not in balance or harmony.

6. Make sure you get enough sleep, exercise or move daily, drink plenty of water and eat healthy.

Detox your body and make it a lifestyle: Please do additional research prior to utilizing any of these suggestions.

- Drink plenty of water.
- Eat garlic, cloves, turmeric, cilantro, parsley, as well as other herbs and spices on a regular basis to help remove toxins from the body.
- Chlorella is a great source to remove mercury and aluminum.
- Eat a healthy diet with lots of vegetables.
- Fasting one morning per week helps eliminate toxins.
- Sweating removes toxins from the skin so exercise regularly, enjoy a sauna or high impact yoga.
- Organic activated charcoal historically has been used to absorb toxins and chemicals. Consuming organic charcoal reduces their toxicity within the body. You can also let charcoal sit on your teeth for a few minutes and it will whiten them.
- Organic Bentonite Clay absorbs toxins, heavy metals, chemicals and impurities within your body. It also has a high concentration of beneficial minerals. It can be used either internally to aid in digestive health or externally as a detox bath or face mask.
- Organic juicing provides a massive amount of vitamins filled with nutrients and helps eliminates toxins from the body.

Metal Detox Juice Recipe:

Wash all and choose organic when possible. For non-organic ingredients, soak in 1 part water to ¼ part vinegar for 10 minutes and rinse.

- 3 large carrots
- 2 large celery stalks
- 1 bunch parsley
- 1 bunch of kale
- 1 large beet
- 1 cucumber
- 2 inches of ginger
- 2 lemons
- 2 apples
- 3 oranges
- 1 Mango

A detoxification bath is relaxing but also helps remove toxins from your body. It is best to do a detox bath prior to bed and may be a helpful for those who have a difficult time sleeping since these baths make you tired. If you struggle with toxins or skin issues this is an inexpensive, easy, natural and gentle recipe:

- 1 cup Baking Soda
- 2 cups Epson Salt or Magnesium Bath Flakes
- 2 cups Apple Cider Vinegar
- Favorite essential oil if desired (Use 10 drops of peppermint or lavender)

Instructions:

- Drink 16 oz. water before drawing a bath.
- Bath should be as hot as you can tolerate and pour ingredients in.
- Bathe at least 15 to 20 minutes or more.
- While bathing drink another 16 oz. glass of water.
- The Detoxification process can make you feel light headed, weak, hot or sweaty.
- After bath, relax on bed and let your body cool down. If you can tolerate drink another 16 oz. of water during sweating.

Essential Oils:

Anything grown from the earth cannot be patented which is why doctors are not trained to suggest alternative healing treatments. Western medicine is a for profit industry. Essential oils have been used for thousands of years and it was common practice for homeopaths to use them to treat their patients. Essential oils can be used without side effects to balance hormones, relieve anxiety, heal skin issues, reduce pain, cleanse the body or just about anything for health and wellbeing. Before using essential oils, not only should you do personal research, you should also consult your doctor if you are taking any prescriptions.

Release Your Junk:

Sit with each of these questions on different days during a meditation session. Stay centered and grounded. Only focus on one per day.

1. What am I afraid of and where do these fears originate? Face your fears by letting them flow through you.

2. What do I blame myself for and what am I most ashamed of? Seek self-forgiveness and self-love by focusing on the present.

3. What disappointments do I have in myself? Find acceptance of past decisions, learn from them, and let them go. Be present. You are no longer your past.

4. What losses in my life am I still grieving about or hanging on to? Holding on to the past keeps us anchored there. Feel your pain fully and let it flow through you so it can be released and you can become centered.

5. What untruths do I tell myself? Always be authentic through self-acceptance, self-love and constant truth.

6. What beliefs or self-dialogue are hampering my growth and development? Open your mind to new concepts and understanding without judgment. Grab what resonates with your truth and discard what doesn't.

7. What am I attached to? Surrender all physical and emotional attachments so that consciousness freely flows. Live in neutrality with compassion and no judgment.

Get to know yourself fully. Meditate on questions about your beliefs, experiences and inner dialogue. Example: You need to have complete control over your circumstances. Ask yourself "Where does this controlling nature originate?", "What will happen if I am not in control in every experience?", "What feelings arise when I think about not having control?" and "How did I feel when I didn't have control as a child?"

Knowing yourself is awareness and awareness raises your energy consciousness. Energy consciousness is what heals and where love and compassion reside.

(1) Neimark, Jill. "The Power of Coincidence." *Psychology Today*. N.p., 03 July 2012. Web. 02

　　　Feb. 2015.

　　　<https://www.psychologytoday.com/articles/200407/the-power-coincidence>.

(2) Myss, Caroline M. *Anatomy of the Spirit: The Seven Stages of Power and Healing*. New

　　　York: Harmony, 1996. Print.

(3) "American Medical Association." - *SourceWatch*. N.p., n.d. Web. 10 Feb.

　　　2015.<http://www.sourcewatch.org/index.php?title=American_Medical_Association>.

(4) Meints, Jeff. "The Hemp Plant, Humankind's Savior." *Understanding the Hemp Plant and Its 50,000 Uses and Benefits!* Understanding the Hemp Plant and Its 50,000 Uses and Benefits!, 23 Jan. 2007. Web. 17 Feb. 2015. <http://www.voteindustrialhemp.com/>.

(5) Anodea, Judith, PH.D. Wheels of Life: A User's Guide to the Chakra System. St. Paul, MN, U.S.A.: Llewellyn Publications, 1987. Print.

(6) "FUCR - Freedom Union & Cannabis Revolution." FUCR - Freedom Union & Cannabis Revolution. N.p., n.d. Web. 13 May 2015.

Chapter 11: The Mind's Effect on Circumstances

"We don't see things as they are; we see things as we are." ~ Anais Nin

According to scientists the average individual has 60,000 thoughts per day and the majority of these are recurring negative thoughts. (1) Our internal dialogue has been conditioned by these thoughts. Constant thought makes it difficult to see through the veil of the minds conditioned fear, distortions, assumptions and judgments. Living in the head perpetuates continual human suffering, simultaneously strengthening the illusion that controlling one's thinking, emotions, health or circumstances is improbable. Difficulties with the power of the mind lie in individual perception preference about obstacles and challenges that are presented daily. Dysfunction or harmony, successes or failures, are determined by how we interpret life experiences. Interpretation is based on choice perception preference.

Constant thought clouds inner awareness. The concept of shutting off the mind seems inconceivable to many because without the mind in action, it appears human beings wouldn't exist as a species without the ability of intelligent thought. Even with a calm mind, intellectual thought is always available when needed. Many people think what goes on in our mind is who they are. Meditation masters reveal higher levels of consciousness beyond the mind's activity. **Without the mind in continual thought, human beings can acquire a higher level of awareness and the ability to see beyond the filtering of our preferred perspectives.** When present and in the moment, our mind is in a calm state of presence, in the state of being present. While being present there is no mind filtering. Our senses become heightened, our creativity is enhanced and we become more accurate about our surroundings and observations.

Collective and individual thoughts are energy. Our thoughts are a mirror of our reality, circumstances and experiences. The "head" creates individual circumstances based on conditioned level of thinking and awareness. Without an awareness of our mind's continual chatter, thinking can produce cycles of stagnant and repetitive behavioral patterns that produce unpleasant life circumstances. Quantum consciousness theory views consciousness as being intrinsically capable of interacting with and altering the physical world generally through quantum interactions, both in the human body at the intracellular level and in the material world at large. (2) The more we know about ourselves internally (self-mastery), the less likely we feel like victims of external factors within our life circumstances.

Every limiting and negative self-concept, belief and accepted falsehood hampers or blocks creative abilities. **Awareness brings light to unconsciousness.** Every creation begins with a clear focused thought (intention). Wishing and hoping does not mold reality. Projecting thoughts of need and lack will create need and lack. With thoughts being energy, a focused intention molds our circumstances or experiences within our reality. Where thought goes our energy flows. With a clear focus and intention through taking action, life no longer becomes the end-result of the many external energy forces that surround our individual circumstances. With awareness, individuals no longer view themselves as victims of life situations.

Millions of people continue to live unaware of their inherited power to alter and create their life circumstances.

Awareness allows us to see the difference between conscious decisions (expect) and unconscious decisions (hope). Utilizing the word "don't" or "want" actively manifests the opposite of what we don't desire because the energy focus is on the core word that is expressed after the "don't" or "want". There is energy behind our words, so it is important to choose them wisely. Instead of focusing on what we don't desire to happen or wanting something, choose words as if you already have it. Wanting something will be just that, a wanting instead of manifesting. **Focusing on words of encouragement, intention and belief that they are already manifested.** Instead of "I want to be healthy", state "I am healthy", even if you are not. Make changes in your life that will manifest health. Intention ultimately elicits control over the external world. When focusing thought and taking action (intention/expect), life no longer becomes the end result of the many external energy forces that surround our circumstances.

Be Present and Be Aware:

Become completely present in everything you do. Even when you need to use your mind for work related activities or projects, be aware of any non-related self-dialogue while completing a task. Being present means your focus is on what you are doing in the now. Practice being present on a daily basis and start with something you enjoy doing so no feelings of dread, boredom or fear arise. Once you become comfortable being present without thought, start being present with something you are less comfortable with. Notice if emotions come in. If there is emotion, notice if there are any thoughts behind the emotion. If not, the emotion is coming from an unconscious conditioning. Meditate on the emotion by putting yourself back in the situation in which you experienced the emotion for the first time. Ask yourself where the emotion is coming from. Sit with it without thought. Let the emotion run its course. You may receive images relating to the emotion and the answer might just pop in your head or synchronicity will bring you the answer in the near future.

Daily Affirmations and Finding Gratitude:

"If you turn it over to the universe you will be surprised and dazzled by what is delivered to you. This is where magic and miracles happen."

~ Joe Vitale

Affirmations are an excellent way to reverse negative thinking patterns. Affirmations are thoughts put into words for the purpose of manifesting intentions. Upon waking each morning start with a couple daily affirmations. They can be as simple as "I am love", "I am wise", or "I am creative". Or more precise such as "I am the creator of my reality therefore I draw abundance, love and compassion". Whatever affirmation you choose, make sure it is only optimistic intentions you desire to draw into your life. Also envision them as something that is already abundant in your life.

"Gratitude unlocks the fullness of life. It turns what we have into enough and more. It turns denial into acceptance, chaos into order and confusion into clarity. It can turn a meal into a feast, a house into

a home, a stranger into a friend. Gratitude makes sense of our past, brings peace for today and creates a vision for tomorrow." ~ Melody Beattie

Create an attitude of gratitude for everything that appears in your life, even something you might consider insignificant. Choosing our thoughts through gratitude puts us in the driver's seat of the mind. Find gratitude in the beauty of a bird or flower. When we create gratitude in our life, we also create abundance. Each time we think or verbalize gratitude we open ourselves up to attaining more of the wonders and beauty of life. Start a daily affirmations and gratitude journal.

"Gratitude draws more things to be grateful for." ~ Renee Cefalu

(1) "Don't Believe Everything You Think." *Stress Free Now*. Cleveland Clinic of Wellness, n.d. Web. 10 Feb.

2015.

http://www.clevelandclinicwellness.com/programs/NewSFN/pages/default.aspx?Lesson=3&Topic=2&UserId=00000000-0000-0000-0000-000000000705>.

(2) Wilber, Ken. *AN INTEGRAL THEORY OF CONSCIOUSNESS* (1197): 71-92. Web. 11 Feb. 2015.

<http://www.imprint.co.uk/Wilber.htm>.

Chapter 12: Education's Effect on the Mind

"Re-examine all you have been told at school or church or in any book, dismiss whatever insults your own soul." ~ Walt Whitman

Instead of teaching youth concepts that prepare them for dealing with real-life issues related to the challenges of life (i.e. social & emotional skills), the K-12 educational system in the United States currently focuses on teaching fundamentals for memorization of information with the main goal of achieving what they deem as intellectual performance. Prioritizing intellectual memorization ability alone has contributed to society's collective consciousness of defining individual self-worth by external factors relating to "mind" intelligence, socioeconomic status, education levels and monetary value. Our education system tends to favor left brain thinkers verses the right brain thinkers which inaccurately defines intelligence since not everyone learns the same way. Visual learners learn through seeing concepts, auditory learners respond to discussion and lectures, while tactile/kinesthetic learners need to be physically involved in learning.

Our education curriculum is based on encouraging students to "always use the head" for retaining as much information as possible relating to external events and facts. Education should be about drawing out creativity, problem-solving and individual uniqueness, not retaining information that will not provide value to the realities of life.

The federal government's "No Child Left Behind Act" ultimately has put enormous pressure on school success by attaching consequences almost exclusively to academic (intellectual) indicators such as test scores (memorization). Interpersonal, visual, emotional, artistic, musical, intuitive, linguistic, logic and spatial intelligences are not recognized, rewarded or even considered as imperative as memorized intelligence. Each child's intelligence is unique and should be fostered as such. *"A deliberate and comprehensive approach to teaching children social and emotional skills can raise grades and test scores, bolster enthusiasm for learning, reduce behavior problems and enhance the brains' cognitive functions."* (1)

"When people hear about issues of "ethical training" or "emotional intelligence training," they tend to think a specific value system is being imposed upon them. Individuals do not recognize that there is already is a value system imposed." ~ Daniel Goleman

"Emotional development precedes most forms of cognitive development; emotional skill-building is a necessary precursor to cognitive skill-building."(1) Teaching youth at the earliest age concepts of the mind and body connection, how thinking creates emotions, how negative emotions affect the physical body and how beliefs formulate the creation of individual circumstance would foster personal responsibility and compassion towards others and the self. Consequently, these skills would help eliminate forms of ignorance fundamentally connected to fear, prejudice and violence. Teaching these concepts in addition to the primary curriculum would provide the momentum for a paradigm shift in awareness of the understanding and correlation of personal responsibility, choice and consequence.

Children are being molded to become productive members within the man-created social structure. They are systematically being conditioned to become members of the work force. They are taught not to question authority, not to think outside the collective mindset and not to question what they are taught. Public school systems contribute to the formulation of titles, roles and socioeconomic value with a bombardment of criticism and negativity if you do not fit in to the conformity plan. Public schools do not encourage differences, creative thinking, problem solving or individuality.

Suppressing a child's individual uniqueness, creativity, and imagination significantly halts or limits that child's ability to grow with confidence and self-worth. A child's authenticity is trampled by the belief that a free thinker won't be accepted by society, a creative out-of-the-box thinker rocks the boat or a thinker that isn't within conformity standards is a threat to the norm. This mindset fuels consciousness dormancy and stifles self-mastery. The collective conditioned mindset contributes to controlling children's self-expression and authenticity.

Lead By Example: Home Tutoring Outside the Classroom

1. Allow children to be their authentic self.
2. Nurture imagination, creativity and problem-solving.
3. Expose your children to art, music, dancing, painting, literature and theater.
4. Support your children's interests and passions.
5. Embrace your child's type of intelligence.

6. Teach personal responsibility, choice and consequence.

7. Teach compassion for others and nature.

8. Teach the importance of truth in action and words.

9. Encourage your child's creative thinking.

10. Support their choices and decisions using guidance where necessary.

11. Never discourage because with failure comes an opportunity for growth.

12. Empower children to find their own solutions.

13. Teach cooperation and how to use dialogue instead of debate.

14. Listen earnestly to what children have to say. You may learn something.

15. Teach your child the skills for meditating. Starting them early will ease painful experiences and childhood challenges.

16. Remind your child to live in the present moment.

17. Regularly let them explore nature.

18. Expose them to classical music and art.

19. Read to your child during pregnancy up until they can read themselves.

20. Encourage daily affirmations.

21. Teach appreciation and gratitude.

22. Remind them to practice their intuitive ability.

23. Teach them how everything said "is all in the delivery". Lead by example.

24. Encourage them to question, with respect, authority or something that doesn't resonate within them or their intuition.

25. Encourage critical thinking and thinking out of the box.

26. Allow children to experience new things.

27. Never take away an experience as a punishment. Experiences are what develops wisdom, self-worth and courage.

The important thing to remember is to allow children to be their authentic self. Authenticity is empowering and it fuels creativity, imagination and acceptance of the self and differences in others without judgment. Embrace originality and authenticity.

(1) Gewertz, C. (2003 Sept). *Hand in Hand.* News Week (p.40)

Chapter 13: Culture's Effect on the Mind

"Do not believe in anything simply because you have heard it. Do not believe in anything simply because it is spoken and rumored by many. Do not believe in anything simply because it is found written in your religious books. Do not believe in anything merely on the authority of your teachers and elders. Do not believe in traditions because they have been handed down for many generations. But after observation and analysis, when you find that anything agrees with reason and is conducive to the good and benefit of one and all, then accept it and live up to it." ~ Buddha

Culture is a collective consciousness more so than individual consciousness. Even though an individual might embrace the collective perception of one's culture, it is the collective that influences the many. The external forces of culture heavily influence beliefs, attitude and behavior. Cultural differences are not organically determined or shaped. **They have been molded by living conditions, resources, environment, location, climate and belief systems.** Culture creates specific behavioral exhibition of dress, facial expressions, values, priorities and emotions. (1) Through generational evolution, culture is altered and improved based on experiences that no longer serve the collective. The collective mindset of culture influences who we are and how we feel, think and behave. Social scientists have identified that one way Western and non-Western cultures differ is the view of the individual self. Without having reverence for all of humanity, individualism can lead to survival of the fittest or take care of your own attitude. Just as collectivistic cultures can contribute to the suppression of individuality because our cultures formulate who we are supposed to be by putting boundaries around personal authenticity.

Each of us is affected by the whole of our culture's collective consciousness. An astounding study done by Princeton University was conducted between August 1998 and November 2003. Seventy five researchers participated in a project that focused on 168 global events. The research found global events created an enormous irregular spike in 37 generators being monitored at the time of these disasters. Over the course of the rest of the day the opposite happened; the generators, as did individuals effected by the disaster, became uncharacteristically quiet and remained unusually quiet for an entire year. The research findings asserted disasters disrupt global consciousness (and machines). Mass demonstrations and celebrations lead to coherent mind field, which shifts these supposedly random machines toward more coherence and "quiet". (2) When many individuals make the same choice collectively, the combined energy of collective consciousness can have an immediate and detectable influence on the larger reality in any environment. (2)(3)

Culture is an expression of a group of people which can divide instead of accept individual differences and the beauty of each of us being inimitable. Every single human is of the collective human race. The only boundaries are those created in our minds. To create "Peace on Earth", there needs to be a collective paradigm shift. People are waking up to government, corporate and political corruption. Global unity is the only way to world peace and prosperity. It is imperative for humanity to come together in unity so that we can take back our inherited freedom of sovereignty from the current system of corporatocracy, a system that holds its own interest above that of the collective human race.

Contribute to the Paradigm Shift:

"Be the change that you wish to see in the world." ~ *Mahatma Gandhi*

A group of people with a collective mindset, goal or focus creates an extremely powerful energy consolidation. Energy flows where there is an intent focus whether it be at a sporting event, celebration or carnival. If we don't stay present and in a neutral stance, we allow our energy to flow into the collective. We are giving our energy source away. It is important to stay grounded at these events so that we keep our physical, emotional and mental space clear and unaffected by the collective.

Change begins within each of us. We have to change ourselves before we can contribute to changing the collective. **With each new person that awakens and focuses their energy on becoming a master of the self, the more powerful the collective becomes for making beneficial changes in families, communities and the system.** We are not on earth to live in our minds. Through raising our consciousness, this realization becomes clear. Consciousness brings everything to light and it becomes easier and easier to create what we desire in our reality. Much of the desired focus becomes helping others and creating a more peaceful existence. With consciousness we experience the connection to everything. We have no desire to judge or harm others in any way. We feel an unconditional compassion and love for all humans and everything associated with life.

What Can You Do?

1. Practice visual meditation to help heal the earth and the suffering of human beings all around the globe.
2. Promote love, unity and peace.
3. Start within yourself. Raise your own level of consciousness or energy frequency. Become the light or catalyst that others will feel and desire to be around.
4. Share what you know.
5. As a daily practice, do something kind for someone else, even if it's a smile.
6. Be present with love and compassion in your words, actions and behaviors.
7. Promote self-care and self-love.
8. Help others when you can.
9. Accept and value others opinions even if they differ from your own.
10. Stop feeding the system.
    - Turn off main stream media
    - Stop consuming things you don't need
    - Live practically
    - Shop locally
    - Take control of your health

(1) Goleman, Daniel. *Destructive Emotions: How Can We Overcome Them?: A*

Scientific Dialogue with the Dalai Lama. New York: Bantam, 2003. Print.

(2) Neimark, Jill. "The Power of Coincidence." *Psychology Today*. N.p., 03 July 2012. Web. 02 Feb. 2015. <https://www.psychologytoday.com/articles/200407/the-power-coincidence>.

(3) Nelson, Roger. "The Global Consciousness Project." *The Global Consciousness Project*. N.p., n.d. Web. 21 July 2015.

Chapter 14: Religion's Effect on the Mind

"This is my simple religion. There is no need for temples; no need for complicated philosophy. Our own brain, our own heart is our temple; the philosophy is kindness." ~ Dalai Lama

Like culture, religions are also a collective consciousness that influence the masses. In most religions, the core concept is love. However, instead of teaching unity, humility and reverence for all life, varied religions throughout the world encourage fear and separation. This simultaneously contributes to isolation from the whole and creates prejudicial thinking of one being better than another. Current religious beliefs fuel division, judgment, discrimination and violence by holding imprecise claims of a superior belief system over other religious beliefs. All religions have the same core values and concepts. However there is little unity between them.

The collective consciousness of culture and religion are closely intertwined. As with culture, religions have a "collective" mind-set that differs from other held beliefs around the world. In July of 2004, Harris Interactive conducted a scientific survey that concluded 69 percent of adult Americans believe the biggest obstacle to world peace is religious differences. As more people are awakening to the injustices around the world, I believe this percentage to be much higher today.

Many religions provide imprecise formulated beliefs rather than encouraging wisdom from within. **Religions have made historical symbolic teachings into a formulated structure of political expectations and obligation.** Similar to cultural norms, many religions have commonly claimed beliefs of how an individual should lead life and in many instances relinquishing personal responsibility through confession. Religions preach love, peace and acceptance. However, world history and the current level of collective consciousness within religions do not necessarily reflect these morals. Throughout the world today, there is increased war, prejudice, disharmony, violence and human suffering.

Discouraging aspects of religions are reflected in the relationship of the teachings of morality. Many religions cling to a belief system which forms individual understanding of a world of separation, superiority, inferiority and righteousness. Religious beliefs are brought into our homes, working environments, communities and political collective consciousness. Beliefs have been formulated by religions and have become rituals to the extent they do not change even when compelling and contradicting information is presented. **Many beliefs cling to stagnancy, a form of dormancy that does not leave room for the progression of change or growth – the evolutionary process.** The simplified route for many is to take another's word for their own truth instead of pursuing the challenging process and conscientious commitment of formulating one's own understanding of life.

Many religions also teach people that human lives are completely destined to God's will. Relinquishing responsibility to "God's choice" or "fate" essentially removes human beings from creating their own life circumstances. *"Whenever individuals seek to avoid responsibility for their own behaviors, they do so with the attempt to give that responsibility and power to some other individual, organization or entity."* (1) God is viewed by many as an entity outside of the self. People are conditioned to believe that all of life (i.e. humans, animals, and nature) are separate from the "whole". This fuels attitudes and behaviors of "survival of the fittest" and "take care of our own". Being separate from the whole encourages behaviors such as prejudice, discrimination, division, destruction of the earth and a collective consciousness of fear.

Life begins when we seek our true essence beyond the conditioned ego. We all are unique individuals with significant purpose. Self-mastery is tapping into your spirituality, seeing beyond the physical. The ancient systems of medicine and healing of the mind, body and spirit were seen as interconnected and non-separable. When one part of the whole (mind, body, spirit) is imbalanced, it affects the other parts. Health in a spiritual perspective concerns all aspects of our physical and emotional being.

Balancing our internal world concurrently balances our external world. Many individuals' belief systems contribute to our past and present state of human existence. Many people live with daily inner chaos. Chaos can be created by imbalanced priorities, guilt, stress and conflicting information regarding spiritual truth and the mind created illusions that devalue others and ourselves. The collective mind-set of the masses living with emotional turmoil creates internal imbalance as well as our external societal and world dysfunction. The more we know ourselves internally, the more personal responsibility becomes a priority and the more we stop placing blame on external factors for the creation of our challenging or unpleasurable circumstances.

Connect with your soul:

1. Question your beliefs. Are your beliefs from experience or are they something that has been handed down from another source? Just because we have been taught something to be the truth doesn't make it our truth.

2. If something doesn't resonate with your intuition, question it... find your own truth.

3. Seek to learn something from everything that happens in your life.

4. Ask for help from God, your higher self or the Universe when seeking assistance or guidance. Look for the synchronicities that appear and direct you to what you're seeking.

5. Never doubt your worth, abilities or purpose in life. When thoughts come in that sabotage you, replace them with an affirmation or find gratitude within your circumstances.

6. Go into any situation with a neutral mindset by refusing to judge others or circumstances. Being present, your mind isn't filtering through your conditioned perception preference.

7. Notice when you are projecting your feelings onto others. Projections are judgments of others and often what we judge in others is a reflection of the same behaviors we possess ourselves.

8. Always use your intuition over your head. Intuition comes directly from your higher self. Do not mistake thoughts for intuition.

9. Practice meditation daily. Meditation raises your level of consciousness through silencing the mind, resulting with an internal stillness.

(1) Buhlman, William. "February 2004 Astral Projection Newsletter." *AstralInfoorg February*

    a.   *2004 Astral Projection Newsletter Comments.* N.p., 12 July 2005. Web. 12 July 2005. <http://www.astralinfo.org/february-2004-obe-newsletter-2.html>.

Chapter 15: The Mind's Creation of Fear

"Fear stifles our thinking and actions. It creates indecisiveness that results in stagnation. I have known talented people who procrastinate indefinitely rather than risk failure. Lost opportunities cause erosion of confidence, and the downward spiral begins." ~ Charles Stanley

The collective consciousness of an individual's family, cultural and religious belief systems contribute to the past and present state of human existence – fear. Fear perpetuates human misery through violence, prejudice and discrimination. Throughout history many individuals live with daily emotional disturbance and inner chaos. Fear is fueled by conflicting information between intuition and the mind's ego.

"Social control is best managed through fear." ~ Michael Crichton

Our society systematically propagates fear. The main tool for spreading fear is through television "programing". Main stream media's focus is on violence, prejudice, separation, scapegoating, oppression, discrimination and war. There are hundreds of thousands of feel good stories to be reported and rarely are. The excuse is that people wouldn't watch it. This is simply propaganda. Everyone loves to hear about human compassion and love. Feel good news always lifts energy frequencies. Most people would prefer uplifting high energy news over fear provoking dense energy broadcasts. We are living in a fear based energy frequency promoted by religion, news outlets and the political landscape.

Varied religious beliefs maintain the notion of an entity called Satan and the after-life of hell or purgatory. Teaching that evil (Satan) is an uncontrollable entity that influences a person's choice removes personal responsibility and generates indisputable fear. Believing in Satan means believing in something outside the "self" that cannot be controlled. Actions of evil are a consequence of a mind conditioned with corrupt and negative thoughts with an underlying factor of fear. These thoughts can be learned through the conditioning of beliefs by those around us or created through physical or emotional harm of violence, neglect or abuse within our life experiences. Fear is an emotion generated by a conscious or unconscious thought. Fear out-of-control generates defense mechanisms and self-destructive behaviors of abuse, obsessions and addictions.

Beliefs about mortality is another issue that fuels fear. The discussion of death is extremely uncomfortable for many, even those who believe there is salvation beyond life. Believing that the purpose of life is to "survive" the persuasion of human sin to avoid hell generates undeniable fear. Near death experiences (NDE) have been encountered by people in exceedingly varied cultural, religious, social, and educational backgrounds. This experience is the closest humans have come to answering the inevitable life occurrence of what happens when the body dies. *Eight million adults in the United States have had an NDE; that is one in twenty.* (1) Individuals who have this experience claim that the level of consciousness an individual has on earth is what they will take with them when their body dies. Each person in a documented case of those who have experienced this phenomenon believes without question that their experience was a real life occurrence. It is explained as consciousness outside of the physical body. Each person's experience differs somewhat in description, however all who experienced NDE come back with the same message. The purpose in life is to love one another.

Another phenomenon that raises question about death is the Out of Body Experience (OBE). As with the NDE, researchers conclude this phenomenon is a separation of consciousness from the body. Surveys show that about 15% to 20% of the population have had an OBE at some time during their life. (2) Meditation masters who can experience the OBE during altered states of consciousness, conclude that this experience is an extraordinary state of awareness outside of the human mind and dualism of the physical world.

Individuals living in a collective imbalance of family, culture, or religion concurrently contribute to societal and world fear disorder. Balancing our internal world simultaneously balances our external world. The more we know about ourselves and our inner dialogue, the less likely it is that we judge or place blame on external factors for creating our challenging or un-pleasurable life circumstances. We have complete control over the steering wheel of life when we attain control over our thinking.

Remove Fear from Your Life:

1. Turn off main stream media and other fear-promoting sources. Five corporations control the mainstream media network. These corporate agendas are not based on fair and investigative journalism. Main stream television programing has become a politically corrupt system based on fear

promoting propaganda. Find alternative news source that investigate to uncover the truth.

"The mainstream media has its own agenda. They do not want to print the facts. They have an agenda, they have a slant, they have a bias..." ~ Curt Weldon

2. Stop watching fear-based movies, television or anything that disturbs your mind-set or lowers your energy vibration. Negativity fuels fear, imbalances the human energy system and triggers neurotransmitters that are detrimental to health.

3. Calm your emotions through breath work. *"A normal human being inhales between 18,000 and 20,000 times per day, totaling an average of 5,000 gallons of air. A normal pair of lungs can hold about two pints of air while the average person breathes in about one pint or less per breath."*(3) Most intellectual activities require so little physical exertion that it leads to shallow breathing. This shallow breathing becomes a habit. Shallow breathing leads to a slower metabolism, lower physical energy levels, less oxygen to the brain, and builds up toxins in the body. In a resting body, one-fourth of the oxygen consumed is used by the brain. The mind can become calmed through a focus on deep breathing. Inhale deeply into your lungs through your nose and exhale through your mouth. Continue until your fear, anxiety or other emotions are released and your mind becomes calm.

"Breath is one of the most powerful tools for transforming

ourselves; for burning up toxins, releasing stored emotions, changing body structure and changing consciousness." ~ Judith Anodea PH.D

4. Move into your heart chakra. **Love and fear cannot share the same space.** Love and fear are opposing ends of the energy spectrum. Fear has a much denser energy than love and it cannot survive in the higher energy space where love resides.

5. Work through your emotional issues such as anger, shame, resentment or guilt. These negative emotions fuel fear.

6. Connect with your soul, the larger part of the self or ego. There is no fear in the soul. The soul is consciousness and with awareness you begin to see through the **illusion of being separate from the whole.**

7. Replace fear with positive affirmations and gratitude.

8. Remember fear is generated by thoughts and thoughts create emotion. When in a fearful place, examine what you are thinking and remind yourself it is not real. The type of fear that is created in the mind has nothing to do with being in danger.

9. Never try to suppress fear for it will resurface more intensely. With every emotion, allow yourself to feel fully and find acceptance so it can move through you. By allowing this to happen, it will dissipate and you gain more power over it.

10. Do research on Tapping (EFT). Tapping is a technique that releases blocked energy meridians in the body and balances our health and wellbeing.

11. Essential oils can release anxiety and promote a sense of calm. The oil frankincense not only helps balance hormones, it also

reduces anxiety and fear. Lavender and lemon supports relaxation and have a calming effect. It is important to research how to apply, inhale or ingest each particular oil. Consult your doctor if you are taking medications.

12. Fear can generate anxiety. Anxiety, depression and other negative emotions have been linked to inactivity and a poor diet. Eat high energy and nutritionally dense foods... living foods.

13. Stay in the present moment. Being present is not allowing your mind to continually race with thoughts.

"Fear keeps us focused on the past or worried about the future. If we can acknowledge our fear, we can realize that right now we are okay. Right now, today, we are still alive, and our bodies are working marvelously. Our eyes can still see the beautiful sky. Our ears can still hear the voices of our loved ones." ~ Thich Nhat Hanh

(1) Moody, Raymond A., and Paul Perry. *The Light beyond*. Toronto: Bantam, 1988. Print.

(2) Blackmore, Susan J. *Beyond the Body: An Investigation of Out-of-Body Experiences*.
London: Heinemann, 1993. Print.

(3) Anodea, Judith, PH.D. Wheels of Life: A User's Guide to the Chakra System. St. Paul, MN, U.S.A.: Llewellyn Publications, 1987. Print.

Chapter 16: Fluoride's Effect on the Mind

Many people think fluoride helps with oral health. Fluoride is a toxin. It is industrial waste from the phosphate industry. Fluoride is the main ingredient in most rodent and bug poisons. It is an accumulate poison that builds up in the bones and the pineal gland. Fluoride has been linked to many health issues including arthritis, bone fractures, allergies, cancer, cardiovascular disease, hypersensitivity, reproductive issues, headaches, kidney disease, GI issues, thyroid disease and brain damage. (1)

Since 1999 over 60 U.S. communities have rejected fluoridation proposals and 98% of Western Europe has rejected fluoridation of their water. (2) Eleven countries that have banned fluoride in their drinking water include Austria, Belgium, China, Denmark, Finland, Germany, Hungary, Japan, Norway, Sweden and the Netherlands. (2)

Yearly, the Poison Control Centers around the US are contacted by thousands due to ingestions of fluoride from dental products. (1) The victims of these poisonings are usually children who have symptoms of vomiting. The Federal Food and Drug Administration (FDA) even requires all fluoride toothpastes must have a poison warning label that reads *"Keep out of reach of children under 6 years of age. If more than used for brushing is accidentally swallowed, get medical help or contact a poison control center right away."*

Until 1999 there had been no research conducted on the impact fluoride has on the pineal gland. The pineal gland regulates the neurotransmitter melatonin and serotonin. Through her research

Dr. Yan Lu concluded that pineal gland is the primary target of fluoride accumulation. She also conducted a study that showed children exposed to fluoride carried a risk of impaired development of intelligence. (3)

Fluoride was first added to drinking water in Nazi Germany concentration camps because it makes people docile. On October 2nd, 1954, chemist Charles Perkins wrote the following to the Lee Foundation for Nutritional Research in Milwaukee, Wisconsin:

"In the 1930s, Hitler and the German Nazis envisioned a world to be dominated and controlled by a Nazi philosophy of pan-Germanism. The German chemists worked out a very ingenious and far-reaching plan of mass control, which was submitted to, and adopted by, the German General Staff. This plan was to control the population in any given area through mass medication of drinking water supplies. By this method they could control the population in whole areas, reduce population by water medication that would induce sterility in women and so on. In this scheme of mass control sodium fluoride occupied a prominent place." ~ Charles Perkins

Fluoride and other toxins in our environment calcify the pineal gland. The pineal gland regulates hormones and sleep rhythms by releasing melatonin during darkness. It is also responsible for the release of the feel good neurotransmitter, serotonin. The pineal gland is located in the center of the brain and is shaped like a pinecone. It is considered the third eye and the seat of the soul. The third eye accesses us to higher levels of consciousness. Ancient Greece believed the pineal gland is the connection into the higher realms of thought. The pineal gland is the connecting link between the physical and higher levels of consciousness or soul.

Detox Your Pineal Gland:

- Educate others and get involved.
- Purchase a reverse osmosis water filtering system and drink more water to help flush toxins.
- Purchase natural toothpaste free of fluoride.
- Eat more organic living earth foods and remove processed foods from your diet.
- Meditate daily with intent to decalcify the pineal gland.
- Detox the body and pineal gland with ginger, lemon, chlorella, apple cider vinegar, cilantro, parsley, iodine supplements and oregano oil.
- Look directly at the sun while soaking up vitamin D. Sungazing should only be done in during sunset and sunrise hours to protect the eyes from stronger sunrays during the day.
- Laughter stimulates the pineal gland.
- Spend more time in nature.
- Limit your exposure to Electromagnetic fields (EMFs). EMFs are invisible frequencies that come from wireless electronic devices. EMFs can produce electromagnetic hypersensitivity including, but not limited to nausea, rashes, headaches and fatigue and tinnitus. (4) Shungite is a mineral that shields EMFs and balances the body's energy.

When people live in total rationality they have a difficult time
freeing themselves to explore things from a different perspective.

~ Renee Cefalu

Self-Mastery Begins With Awareness.

Working through emotions begins with questioning beliefs and learning to reverse destructive thinking patterns. Only we are responsible for every aspect of ourselves. It no longer serves human beings to place blame on others for our personal reactions, behaviors or emotions. Self-awareness is the process of letting go of regrets, shame, blame, resentment, hatred and beliefs that are self-defeating and destructive to our overall health and well-being. To be in harmony with your mind and body and life itself, it is a necessity to let go of the illusion of being a victim of our circumstances. To embrace your authentic you, you must free yourself from dense energy that comes from harboring emotions and feelings that no longer serve you in the present moment. This process of self-mastery never ends, however with each new experience comes a deeper understanding, an acquired wisdom, an inner contentment.

Mastering the self is simply "I am" at any given time just "being" in the present moment as the "self". When being present there is no need for titles, labels or defining oneself as something external. When being in the present you just live in each and every moment in neutrality while holding an energy frequency of love and compassion.

To truly know oneself is like an oak tree planted deeply in the soil unwavering, strong and solid. No force can move you beyond the wisdom of your inner strength or from the magnitude of your worthiness to live in purpose of your true nature on this earth.

End Note:

We are fortunate to live in a part of the world that offers adequate resources to survive life in comfort. Other parts of the world human beings are suffering with endless government suppression, censorship, lack of vital resources, violence and war. The information in this book obviously would be worthless when in constant survival mode. This book is for those who have adequate resources. It's time to contribute to a paradigm shift to heal the world. It begins with every person who awakens to their innate birthright of living in health and harmony through the endless process of "Self Mastery".

(1) "Fluoride Action Network." *Fluoride Action Network*. N.p., n.d. Web. 10 Feb.

2015. <http://fluoridealert.org/issues/health/>.

(2) "Fluoride Action Network." *Fluoride Action Network*. N.p., n.d. Web. 08 Feb.

2015. <http://fluoridealert.org/issues/water/>.

(3) Lu, Yan, Dr. "EFFECT OF HIGH-FLUORIDE WATER ON INTELLIGENCE IN

CHILDREN." Academia.edu, n.d. Web. 01 Apr. 2015.

<http://www.academia.edu/8957948/EFFECT_OF_HIGH-

FLUORIDE_WATER_ON_INTELLIGENCE_IN_CHILDREN>.

(4) "Electromagnetic Hypersensitivity – Symptoms, Prevention and Recovery."

Electromagnetic Hypersensitivity – Symptoms, Prevention and

Recovery. N.p., n.d. Web. 10 Feb. 2015. <http://www.best-emf-

health.com/electromagnetic-hypersensitivity.html>.

Works Cited

Ackerman, Diane. An Alchemy of Mind: The Marvel and Mystery of the Brain. New

York: Scribner, 2004. Print.

"About Neurotransmitters." BrainChemical.com. N.p., 2005. Web. 2005.

<http://www.brainchemical.com/about-neurotransmitters.asp>.

"American Medical Association." - SourceWatch. N.p., n.d. Web. 10 Feb. 2015.

<http://www.sourcewatch.org/index.php?title=American_Medical_Asso

ciation>.

Anodea, Judith, PH.D. Wheels of Life: A User's Guide to the Chakra System. St. Paul,

MN, U.S.A.: Llewellyn Publications, 1987. Print.

Blackmore, Susan J. Beyond the Body: An Investigation of Out-of-Body Experiences.

London: Heinemann, 1993. Print.

Blake, Kati. "Nutritional Deficiencies (Malnutrition)." Healthline. George Krucik, MD, 26

July 2012. Web. 12 Feb. 2015.
<http://www.healthline.com/health/malnutrition#Symptoms4>.

Boeree, George C. "Personality Theories." Carl Jung. N.p., 1997. Web. 12 July 2005.

<http://www.ship.edu/~cgboeree/jung.html>.

Bryson, Christopher. The Fluoride Deception. New York: Seven Stories, 2004. Print.

Buhlman, William. "February 2004 Astral Projection Newsletter." AstralInfoorg February

2004 Astral Projection Newsletter Comments. N.p., 12 July 2005. Web. 12 July
2005. <http://www.astralinfo.org/february-2004-obe-newsletter-2.html>.

Chopra, Deepak. Ageless Body, Timeless Mind: The Quantum Alternative to Growing

Old. New York: Harmony, 1993. Print.

Chopra, Deepak. The Book of Secrets: Unlocking the Hidden Dimensions of Your Life.

New York: Harmony, 2004. Print.

Connett, Michael. "Fluoride Action Network." *Fluoride Action Network*. N.p., Mar.

2012. Web. 10 Feb. 2015. <http://fluoridealert.org/studies/acute03/>.

"Don't Believe Everything You Think." *Stress Free Now*. Cleveland Clinic of Wellness,

n.d. Web. 10 Feb. 2015.

<http://www.clevelandclinicwellness.com/programs/NewSFN/pages/de

fault.aspx?Lesson=3&Topic=2&UserId=00000000-0000-0000-0000-

000000000705>.

"Electromagnetic Hypersensitivity – Symptoms, Prevention and Recovery."

Electromagnetic Hypersensitivity – Symptoms, Prevention and Recovery.

N.p., n.d. Web. 10 Feb. 2015. <http://www.best-emf-

health.com/electromagnetic-hypersensitivity.html>.

"Fluoride Action Network." *Fluoride Action Network*. N.p., n.d. Web. 08 Feb. 2015.

<http://fluoridealert.org/issues/water/>.

"Fluoride Action Network." *Fluoride Action Network*. N.p., n.d. Web. 10 Feb. 2015.

<http://fluoridealert.org/issues/health/>.

"FUCR - Freedom Union & Cannabis Revolution." FUCR - Freedom Union & Cannabis

Revolution. N.p., n.d. Web. 13 May 2015.

Gero, Glenn B., N.D.,D.Sc., R.H. (AHG), M.E.S., C.L.C. "Neurotransmitter Level Testing."

*New Jersey Holistic Health, NJ Alternative Medicine: Neurotransmitter

Testing*. N.p., n.d. Web. 10 Feb. 2015.

<http://www.holisticnaturopath.com/neurotrans.htm>.

Gewertz, C. (2003 Sept). *Hand in Hand*. News Week (p.40)

Goleman, Daniel. *Destructive Emotions: How Can We Overcome Them?: A Scientific

Dialogue with the Dalai Lama*. New York: Bantam, 2003. Print.

Golubic, Mladen, MD, PhD. "Lifestyle Choices: Root Causes of Chronic Diseases."

    Cleveland Clinic. N.p., 14 Jan. 2013. Web. 10 Feb. 2015.

    <http://my.clevelandclinic.org/health/transcripts/1444_lifestyle-choices-

    root-causes-of-chronic-diseases>.

Gothard, Katalin, MD, PhD, Evan Carr, BS, Shih-pi Ku, PhD, and Sebastian Korb, PhD.

    "News Releases Archives." *Society for Neuroscience*. N.p., 14 Oct. 2012.

    Web. 10 Feb. 2015. <http://www.sfn.org/Press-Room/News-Release-

    Archives/2012/New-Research-Reveals-More-About-How-the-Brain-

    Processes-Facial-Expressions-and-Emotions?returnId=%7B0C16364F-DB22-

    424A-849A-B7CF6FDCFE35%7D>.

"ISTPP: The Congressional Prevention Coalition." *ISTPP: The Congressional Prevention*

    Coalition. N.p., n.d. Web. 10 Feb. 2015.

    <http://istpp.org/coalition/stress_prevention.html>.

Kallen, B. (2002, July). *Power of Optimism*. Men's Fitness, 34(3). Retrieved January

    26, 2003 from the World Wide Web: http://web5.infotrac-

    college.com/wadsworth/session/1/397/56712780/19!xrn_18_0_A8858'

King, M. *Medical Biochemistry Neurotransmitters - Human Physiology* (p.209).

    Retrieved July 12, 2005 from the World Wide Web:

    http://web.indstate.edu/thcme/mwking/nerves.html

Korn, Joey. "Messages from Water." *Spiritual Dowsing*. N.p., 1997. Web. 12 July 2005.

    <http://www.dowsers.com/dr-masaru-emotos-messages-from-water/>.

Lu, Yan, Dr. "EFFECT OF HIGH-FLUORIDE WATER ON INTELLIGENCE IN

    CHILDREN." Academia.edu, n.d. Web. 01 Apr. 2015.
    <http://www.academia.edu/8957948/EFFECT_OF_HIGH-
    FLUORIDE_WATER_ON_INTELLIGENCE_IN_CHILDREN>.

Mayo Clinic Staff. "Meditation." : *Take a Stress-reduction Break Wherever You Are*.

  N.p., 19 July 2014. Web. 11 Feb. 2015. <http://www.mayoclinic.org/tests-
  procedures/meditation/in-depth/meditation/art-20045858>.

Meints, Jeff. "The Hemp Plant, Humankind's Savior." *Understanding the Hemp Plant*

  and Its 50,000 Uses and Benefits! Understanding the Hemp Plant and Its
  50,000 Uses and Benefits!, 23 Jan. 2007. Web. 17 Feb. 2015.
  <http://www.voteindustrialhemp.com/>.

Myss, Caroline M. *Anatomy of the Spirit: The Seven Stages of Power and Healing*.

  New York: Harmony, 1996. Print.

Myss, Caroline M., and C. Norman Shealy. *The Creation of Health: The Emotional,*

  Psychological, and Spiritual Responses That Promote Health and Healing.
  New York: Three Rivers, 1998. Print.

Moody, Raymond A., and Paul Perry. *The Light beyond*. Toronto: Bantam, 1988. Print.

Neimark, Jill. "The Power of Coincidence." *Psychology Today*. N.p., 03 July 2012.

  Web. 02 Feb. 2015.
  <https://www.psychologytoday.com/articles/200407/the-power-
  coincidence>.

Nelson, Roger. "The Global Consciousness Project." *The Global Consciousness*

  Project. N.p., n.d. Web. 21 July 2015.

NewsRX. "Thinking Positively About Aging Extends Life More than Exercise and Not

  Smoking." *Yale News*. Stanislav Kasi/Martin Slade/Suzannie Kunkel, 29 July
  2002. Web. 02 Feb. 2015. <http://news.yale.edu/2002/07/29/thinking-
  positively-about-aging-extends-life-more-exercise-and-not-smoking>.

Sargent, Allen C. *The Other Mind's Eye: The Gateway to the Hidden Treasures of*

Your Mind. Malibu, CA: Success Design International Publications, 1999.
Print.

Storer, Bev. "How Stress Effects Neurotransmitters." *» Stress*. N.p., 02 July 2009. Web. 12
July 2005. <http://www.stress-anxiety-
depression.org/stress/neurotransmitters.html>.

Tolle, Eckhart. *The Power of Now: A Guide to Spiritual Enlightenment*. Novato, CA:
New World Library, 1999. Print.

"Thinking Positively About Aging Extends Life More than Exercise and Not Smoking."
Yale News. N.p., 29 July 2002. Web. 10 Feb. 2015.
<http://news.yale.edu/2002/07/29/thinking-positively-about-aging-
extends-life-more-exercise-and-not-smoking>.

Ullman, Dana. *Discovering Homeopathy: Medicine for the 21st Century*. Berkeley,
CA: North Atlantic, 1988. Print.

Wilber, Ken. *AN INTEGRAL THEORY OF CONSCIOUSNESS* (1197): 71-92. Web. 11 Feb.
2015. <http://www.imprint.co.uk/Wilber.htm>.

Made in the USA
Middletown, DE
20 August 2015